DEDICATION

To all the extraordinary Knitting Tree customers. Thanks for sharing your desire and passion for knitting, your wit and humor, and your wonderful accomplishments.

ACKNOWLEDGMENTS

Hugs and kisses to Margery Rosenthal, who got me into this wonderful addiction; Midge Varren, who taught me fine finishing; Ute Kowalski, who was my partner in crime and forced me to master the shrimp stitch. Thank you Patsy Tompkins and Karen Wilder for pushing me forward. To all my New York knitters, God bless you for all your encouragement. Thank you Adina Klien, Petra Marcelle, and Irnina Poludneinko for keeping me in love, laughter, and yarn.

To my new extended family at the Knitting Tree, thanks for keeping me going and having faith in my creativity. You guys are awesome. A special thanks to Olga Pobedinskaya, for being my extra set of hands. Most of all I want to "thank you skeins for purling me into a new level of happiness and knitting bliss." Knit on!

—Melissa

From left to right: Jolene, Liz, Melissa and Trooper, Eileen, Marcy, and Sheryl.

Contents

Meet Melissa

MELISSA HAS BEEN DESIGNING and knitting basically brilliant garments for more than twenty-five years. She is known for leaving her shop, the Knitting Tree, on a Saturday afternoon with a bag of yarn under her arm and returning Tuesday morning wearing a new sweater. Her creativity and inspired sense of flair seem endless. At times, her sense of humor almost exceeds her imagination for knitting designs.

Well known for her design capabilities, Melissa is regularly commissioned by top international yarn manufacturers to design superb knitwear garments. Knitting Tree customers can choose from more than five hundred house patterns or get a custom design on the spot. Others know Melissa only from her Web page, www.knittingtree.com.

This book contains a little of Melissa that you too can enjoy. Look for the Melissa's Point boxes and tap into her abundant humor and knack for the dramatic. The Skill Builder sections signal a mini knitting lesson and provide valuable information to help perfect your knitting technique.

Knit Melissa's basically brilliant designs and enjoy her sense of humor. And the next time you're in Madison, Wisconsin, treat yourself. Stop by the Knitting Tree and meet Melissa in person.

Before You Begin

OBTAINING A GOOD FIT need not be a challenge. Fit and comfort are personal matters. Since you are in control of your knitting, knit the garment with the fit you prefer. To obtain a good fit, there are a few important components you need to work with. Combining these components with the correct pattern size will result in a finished product that fits. These components include:

- Taking body measurements

- Making a gauge swatch

- Measuring your knitting

taking body measurements

BUY A GOOD FLEXIBLE tape measure—no, your husband's metal tape measure won't work. Measure across the largest part of the bust. This is usually the measurement that determines which size to knit. Then measure across the largest part of the hips. This measurement is less critical unless you're making a long garment or if your hips are larger than your bust.

BODY MEASUREMENTS

- Bust _____

- Hips _____

- Desired length of garment _____

- Circumference of wrist _____

- Circumference of upper arm _____

- Desired length of sleeve _____

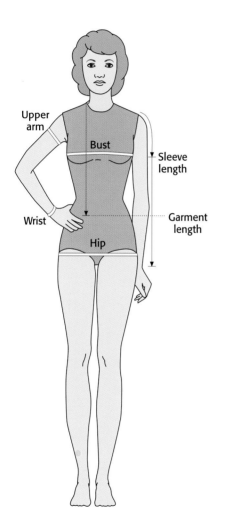

Upper
arm

Bust

Sleeve
length

Wrist

Garment
length

Hip

melissa's point

I hate measuring my hips, but
I would rather knit than exercise.

Make sure the width of the garment accommodates the larger measurement: bust or hips. Next measure the circumference of your wrist and upper arm, then the desired length of the sleeve. For the most flattering fit, don't let the bottom of the sweater fall at the widest part of your body. Determine where you would like it to end, either above or below the widest part. Hold the tape measure at the top of your shoulder and note the desired length. Check the pattern and lengthen or shorten the garment to the length most flattering for you.

You are now ready to select the correct size of pattern. Don't rely on the name small, medium, or large; they are just guidelines. Look at the finished bust measurements given for each pattern. Compare the finished measurements with your body measurements, adding several inches for comfort. The number of additional inches is a matter of personal taste. For a close-fitting garment, add 1" to 3". For a more classic fit, add 4" to 6". And for an oversized fit, add 6" to 10+".

Measuring a favorite sweater is also a good way to determine which size to make. Comparing the measurements of a favorite sweater with your body measurements will give you an idea of the amount of ease you prefer in a garment; measuring the length will help determine how long to make your sweater.

making a gauge swatch

GAUGE IS NOT A dirty word. The reason for doing a gauge is simply to determine the number of stitches per inch. This number is required to predict the measurements of the piece you knit. Not everyone does a gauge. Melissa doesn't always do a gauge, but as a shop owner and designer, she makes samples. If the sweater turns out tiny, it's a Small; if it's huge, it's an Extra Large. Others who don't do a gauge believe in "knit and give." Knit the garment, and then give it to someone who fits into it.

However, if you want the garment to fit, accept the fact that you will have to do a gauge, and begin the swatch process.

The needle size given should be considered as a starting point only. It doesn't matter what needle size you use, what matters is that you obtain the correct gauge. It may take several attempts with different needles to get the correct gauge.

Make a swatch using the yarn you plan to use for the project. If your sweater is done in a pattern stitch, your swatch should have enough stitches to work across the pattern. If your sweater is done in stockinette stitch, cast on about 4" worth of stitches. The gauge noted in the pattern or on the yarn label will give an indication of how many stitches that is. Cast on and work in pattern for several inches.

Measure the width of the piece while it's still on the needles. Divide the number of stitches on the needle by the width of the swatch. If the number of stitches per inch is larger than you want, try a larger needle size. For example, if you want 4 stitches to 1" and you have 4.5 stitches, go up a needle size. If the number of stitches per inch is less than you want, go down a needle size. Continue to make swatches using a different needle size until you have the correct gauge.

Being close is a disaster waiting to happen; you want to be exact. Working 77 stitches at 3.5 stitches per inch will result in a piece measuring 22" across, but at 3.8 stitches

per inch, the piece will only be 20¼". The result is a snug little sweater when you wanted a boxy, comfortable fit.

measuring your knitting

IT IS IMPORTANT to measure your knitting numerous times as you work. Spread the stitches out across the needle and lay them on a tabletop or other smooth surface. Don't smooth the knitting over a carpet to measure. The yarn may "stick" to the carpet fibers and distort the measurements. Let the stitches move freely. Don't tug or stretch the piece—that's cheating. To measure the width, measure from side to side, unrolling the edges as necessary. To measure the length, place the tip of the tape measure below the needle.

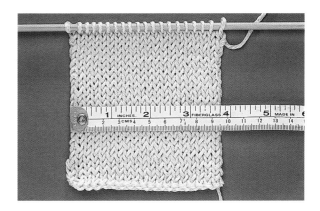

To measure width, unroll edges as necessary.

To measure length, place tape below needle.

making adjustments and alterations

NOW THAT YOU HAVE all the components, put all the calculations together and determine if any adjustments to the pattern are necessary. Refer to the pattern and accompanying diagram. Select the pattern size that gives enough ease to comfortably cover your widest part—bust or hips.

The length of a garment is easy to adjust, but must be done before reaching the armhole. To shorten the length, eliminate the appropriate number of inches before reaching the armhole. To lengthen the piece, add the appropriate number of inches before reaching the armhole. The armhole length will not be affected by this change, but the entire length of the piece will be. Make note of the adjustments on the pattern so that the front and back pieces will be adjusted by the same amount.

If you are rather busty and find that your sweaters usually ride up in the front, adjust the length of the front only. Add 2" to the length of the front, again before reaching the armholes. Yes, the front will now be 2" longer than the back. When sewing the pieces together, ease these extra inches evenly along the side seam. When you wear the sweater, the added length of the front will not be apparent and the fit will be much more pleasing.

Adjustments to the sleeve length need to be done before shaping the sleeve cap. An easy way to determine when to start the sleeve cap is to hold the knit sleeve up to your arm. When the sleeve is long enough to reach the top of the bra at the underarm, begin shaping the cap.

selecting yarns

TODAY'S KNITTER HAS A tremendous range of yarns to work with. Words like exquisite, irresistible, alluring, glamorous, comforting, and enticing are often used to describe yarn. Few things in life compare with the thrill of starting a project and working with new yarn. Be careful—yarn can be addictive.

The garments in this collection are made from a variety of yarns and you may want to choose the actual yarn suggested in the directions. Each season, however, manufacturers bring new yarns to market and retire older yarns. Experiment to find the perfect substitute, or create your own yarn.

melissa's point
Measure often as you knit, especially if you drink. Measure once if drinking iced tea (and I'm not talking Long Island iced tea). Measure twice if drinking a glass of wine. Measure three times if drinking a martini— and put away the knitting.

SUBSTITUTING YARNS

When selecting yarn for your project, you may find that the suggested yarn is no longer available or that you'd rather find something else to create your own custom look. You can substitute yarns easily as long as you remember to find a yarn that matches the gauge stated in the pattern.

COMBINING YARNS

One way to create your own custom look is by combining yarns. Working two yarns together throughout will give the impression of a new yarn with a totally different look. Combining yarns may also be necessary to bulk up thinner yarns to achieve a specific gauge. The guidelines in the following chart will help in your selection. Do a swatch to be sure of your gauge.

GUIDE FOR COMBINING YARNS

Yarn Combinations	Approximate New Gauge
Two DK weight yarns	= 3.5 sts per inch
One DK yarn and one worsted yarn	= 3 sts per inch
Two worsted yarns	= 2.75 sts per inch

For a rag look, combine two flat, solid colors. Combining a flat and a textured or slubbed yarn makes an interesting new yarn and is a Melissa favorite. Using two textured yarns will yield a different yarn with new depth, but be careful: this may be overkill.

Never be afraid of mixing colors that at first glance don't match. The result may be pleasantly surprising. Go ahead and experiment; try yarns that you would not usually put together. To see how the yarns look when combined, pull out a 10" piece of each of the yarns, twist them together and then wrap them around your finger. If it's incredible, go with it; if it's not, try another combination. Don't forget to knit a gauge swatch to make sure that the gauge matches the gauge called for in the garment and that you like the results of the combined yarns.

Knitting Know-How

KNITTING IS AN ART FORM and the knitter is the artist. Completing a project gives knitters an enormous sense of achievement. Swell with pride when the compliments come rolling in.

Assuming you have the basic knitting skills—that is, you know how to cast on, knit, purl, and bind off—you are ready to begin. As with any art form, your skill level increases the more you practice.

yes, you can knit it

MELISSA IS FAMOUS FOR telling her customers, "Yes you can knit it." A sweater may look elaborate and impressive, but that does not mean it comes with a difficult set of instructions. The skill level is indicated for each of the patterns. Many are quick and easy to make, even for beginners. Only a moderate degree of knitting skill is required to successfully complete any of the sweaters in this collection. Each pattern has a Skill Builder box that provides an additional suggestion or two for adding to your knitting knowledge.

Reading knitting patterns is like eating an elephant, one bite at a time. You may not understand some sections when you first read through the entire pattern. This is common. But when you read a sentence, and then knit as directed and work your way through a pattern, the next step will become more apparent.

Directions for different sizes are in parentheses ( ). If only one number appears, it applies to all sizes. To avoid confusion, you may want to circle or highlight the numbers that apply to the size you are making.

reading stitches

KNITTERS HAVE DEVISED MANY ways to keep track of their knitting. Some use gadgets to help them keep count; others write notes as they go. Both of these methods require the additional step of recording. A simpler method is to become familiar with and understand your knitting. By recognizing the knit stitches and the purl stitches, you can keep track of your progress. A close look at your knitting will reveal the different stitches; learn to recognize the increases and the decreases.

When working a pattern stitch, look at your work: how the stitch lies, how it looks on the front and on the back. Whenever the pattern is repeated, glance at your knitting. Check cables after completing the twist row to be sure they all twist the correct way; it's a real bummer to notice mistakes 3" later. If the stitches look fine, knit on. If the stitches are not right, fix the error before proceeding. Or put that project down and pick up project number two. Melissa feels one should have at least two projects going at all times.

Knit and Purl stitches

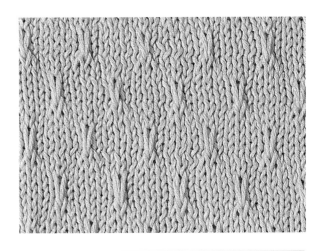

Pattern stitches

Cable stitches

Finishing

DON'T SKIMP ON THE finishing of your sweaters. Spend a few extra minutes on the finishing touches, and you will have a beautiful and professional-looking sweater. Skimp, and the best you can hope for is mediocre.

crochet edges

ADDING CROCHET EDGING around a garment is simple to do and adds a special touch to a knit garment. Always start with a foundation row of single crochet, worked on the right side. Beware of putting stitches too close to the edge, which can cause puckering. The method is different than picking up stitches for knitting. When done correctly, the edge should lie flat and hardly needs to be blocked.

The formula for a vertical row edge is one single crochet every other row. Melissa explains it this way, "Into the knot, only into the knot."

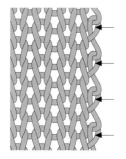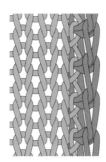

Crochet into every knot.

The formula for the horizontal bind-off edge is one single crochet every 1½ stitches. Go into a stitch, then between the next two stitches, and repeat across the row.

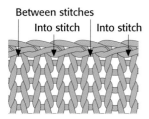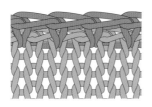

Between stitches
Into stitch | Into stitch

The *shrimp stitch* (or reverse single crochet) is often used in this book and gives a nice braided edge. First, work a foundation row of single crochet. Without turning your work, work another row of single crochet in reverse. Work left to right, inserting the hook into the stitch below, and complete the single crochet.

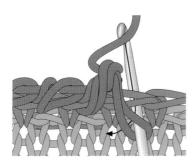

knit edges

MANY KNITTERS PREFER to finish the edges of a garment by knitting them. To do this, you need to pick up stitches for the neckband, and if it's a cardigan, for the front bands. The pattern may or may not tell you how many stitches to pick up. Either way, the goal is the same—to pick up stitches evenly along the edges of the garment. Always pick up stitches with the right side facing you unless instructed otherwise.

Use the following formulas to help distribute the stitches evenly along the edges.

The formula for picking up stitches on the neck edge of a pullover, starting at the right shoulder seam, is to pick up one stitch in every stitch all the way around the bound-off edge. For a vertical edge of a cardigan, you will need to adjust the number of stitches to pick up to account for the difference between the stitch gauge and the row gauge. In general, the stitch gauge is one less number than the row gauge. For example, a stitch gauge of four stitches per inch will probably have a row gauge of five rows per inch.

The formula for picking up stitches on a front edge is: *pick up the number of stitches in the row gauge, skip one stitch, repeat from * along the front edge. Using our example of four stitches per inch and five rows per inch, you would start at the bottom of the center front and pick up five stitches, one per row; then skip one row and repeat until you reach the front neck edge. Along the neck, pick up one stitch in every stitch as for the pullover neck edge.

When working in a rib or garter stitch pattern, use a needle size smaller than the one used for the body of the sweater. When doing a pattern stitch, the number of stitches to be picked up needs to be evenly divided by the stitch repeat. For example, a knit-two, purl-two rib is a four-stitch repeat, so the number of stitches picked up will have to be evenly divided by four. Melissa works the first round and either adds a stitch or knits two together to get the correct number.

Along neck edges, pick up one stitch per stitch and continue in established rib pattern.

closures

BUTTONS AND ZIPPERS are good options for keeping the fronts of cardigans and jackets closed. They can also be used to embellish and enhance the appearance of a garment. Changing the size and number of buttons can dramatically change the overall look.

BUTTONS AND BUTTONHOLES

First, determine the size and number of buttons you want. An odd number of buttons seems to be more pleasing than an even number. Melissa's grandmother always told her to use an odd number, just like the petals on flowers.

Second, determine the size of the buttonhole. A button ⅝" or smaller may not require a buttonhole. The button can probably slip between the stitches. A 1" button requires a one-stitch buttonhole. Larger buttons require a two-or-more-stitch buttonhole. Remember the yarn and buttonhole stretch. The buttonhole should hold the button snugly. If the hole is too loose and the button doesn't stay closed, hand stitch one end of the buttonhole closed.

Determine the desired width of your button band and work the buttonholes one row closer to the picked-up edge than the center; this will provide a more stable buttonhole band. To determine how far apart to work the buttonholes, use the formula that follows. The example shows how to calculate the number of stitches between two-stitch buttonholes for five buttonholes, with three stitches at the top and three stitches at the bottom.

Picked-up stitches on button band 80

Stitches above top button . . . . −3

Stitches below bottom button . . . . −3

Number of stitches required for buttonholes

(5 buttons x 2 stitches per buttonhole) − 10

= 64

Number of stitches between buttonholes

(64 divided by 4 segments*) = 16

The number of segments is the number of buttons minus 1.

For a one-stitch buttonhole: work required stitches at top, *work the number of stitches determined from the buttonhole formula, yarn over, knit two together, repeat from *, end with required stitches at bottom.

For a two-stitch buttonhole: work required stitches at top, *work the number of stitches determined from the buttonhole formula, slip two, pass the first slipped stitch over the second, slip another stitch, pass slipped stitch over the last one slipped, slip remaining slipped stitch back to left needle, cast on two stitches, repeat from *, end with required stitches at bottom.

For a larger buttonhole: follow directions for the two-stitch buttonhole, slipping and passing over as many stitches as necessary and remembering to cast back on the same number of stitches.

ZIPPERS

Another option for closing a sweater or jacket is with a zipper. Buy a zipper that is ½" to 1" shorter than the opening.

Work a single row of crochet to provide a smooth edge on which to sew the zipper. Working from the front of the garment, with the zipper closed, pin the zipper in place using straight pins, easing the edge carefully to avoid puckers. Check to be sure the upper and lower edges of the garment are even and the pieces hang straight. Using a sewing needle and matching-colored thread, baste into place. The basting can stay in place if it is neatly done. Turn the garment inside out and whipstitch the edges of the zipper to the garment. Reinforce the top and bottom of the zipper with a few extra stitches to secure these stress points on the zipper.

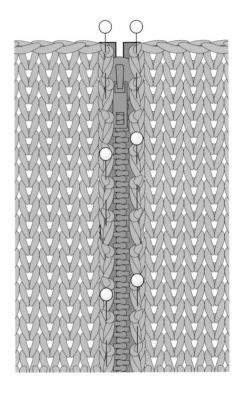

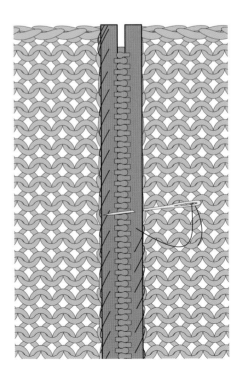

blocking

BLOCKING WILL SMOOTH OUT most irregularities and help in the final shaping of your garment. Most novelty or fancy yarns don't need to be blocked. Stitches knit with flat yarns may appear uneven unless blocked. Blocking after the garment is completed will also help soften the seams.

Set your iron to the highest setting. While it is heating up, wet a hand towel and wring it out. Spread a dry towel on a flat surface and pin the garment, carefully shaping it to the desired measurements. Cover the garment with the wet hand towel. With the iron, ever so gently, lower it as close to the towel as you can without making contact. You will hear "pstttt" and see it steam. But never, never let the weight of the iron touch the garment.

At the Knitting Tree, Melissa has a professional steam iron that is fondly referred to as the Magic Iron. Melissa has been known to work miracles for those who didn't carefully measure their gauge by adjusting the width or length of knit pieces with the Magic Iron. You too can do miracles, but start carefully and work cautiously.

Blocked

Unblocked

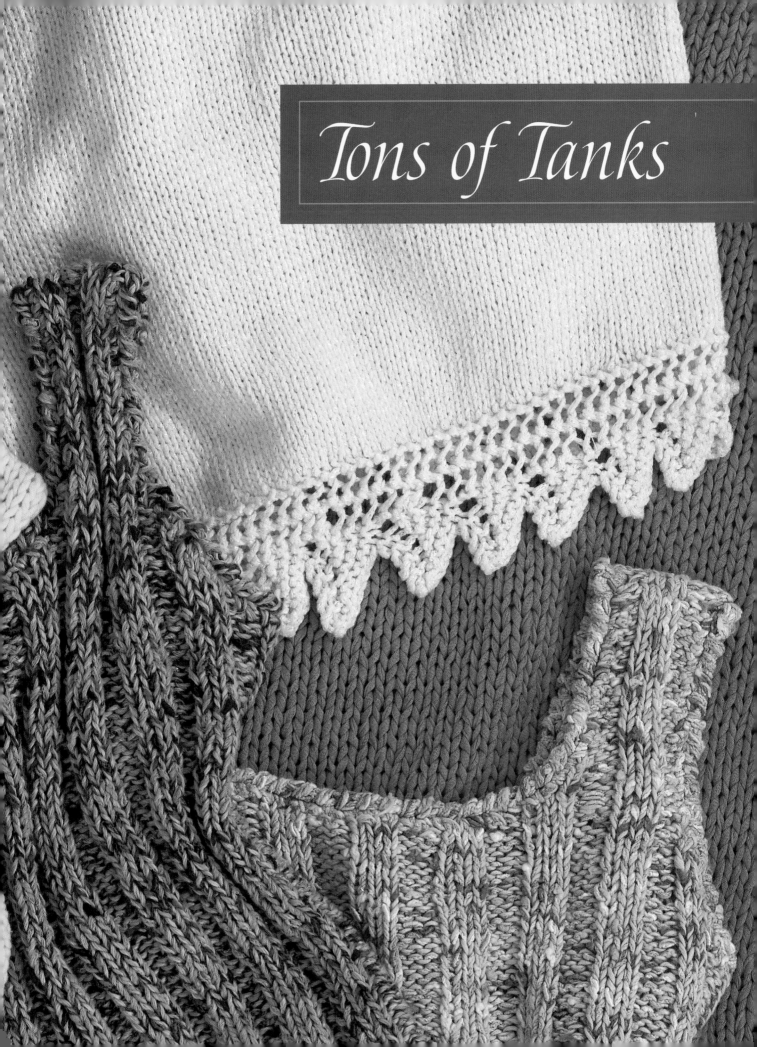

Tons of Tanks

Shark Fin Tank

This tank top has an elegant drape and knit lace hem.
Crochet edges provide a refined, feminine look.

Skill Level: Intermediate

Sizes: Extra Small (Small, Medium, Large)

Finished Bust Measurements: 32 (35, 38½, 41½)"

materials

- 5 (6, 6, 7) skeins Muench String of Pearls (70% cotton, 20% viscose, 10% polyester; 99 yds/skein), color 4010

- Size 8 needles (or size required to obtain gauge)

- Size G crochet hook

GAUGE: 20 sts and 24 rows = 4" in St st

---

melissa's point
The bottom lace is really very easy to knit. Worked side to side,
it's simply garter stitch and YOs. Try it.

 ## skill builder

RATHER THAN HAVE KNOTS in the middle of your garment, tie on a new ball of yarn at the beginning of a row. To determine how much yarn is needed to get across a row, lay the work flat; then measure out enough yarn to reach across the work 2½ times for Stockinette stitch. If you don't have enough, tie on a new ball of yarn and leave about a 4" tail so that you can weave the tail into the seams.

lace border

CO 8 sts. Knit 1 row. Work patt as follows:

Row 1 (RS): Sl 1 wyib, K1, (YO, K2tog) twice, YO, K2—9 sts.

Row 2: K2, YO, K2, (YO, K2tog) twice, K1—10 sts.

Row 3: Sl 1 wyib, K1, (YO, K2tog) twice, K2, YO, K2—11 sts.

Row 4: K2, YO, K4, (YO, K2tog) twice, K1—12 sts.

Row 5: Sl 1 wyib, K1, (YO, K2tog) twice, K4, YO, K2—13 sts.

Row 6: K2, YO, K6, (YO, K2tog) twice, K1—14 sts.

Row 7: Sl 1 wyib, K1, (YO, K2tog) twice, K6, YO, K2—15 sts.

Row 8: BO 7 sts, K3 (including st already on needle), (YO, K2tog) twice, K1—8 sts.

Rep rows 1–8 until border measures 16 (17, 19, 21)". BO all sts.

back

On straight edge of border piece, PU 80 (88, 96, 104) sts and work in St st until piece measures 9 (10½, 12, 13½)" excluding border. **Shape armholes:** BO 4 (4, 5, 6) sts at beg of next 2 rows, BO 2 (2, 4, 4) sts at beg of next 2 rows, dec 1 st at each edge EOR 4 (5, 5, 6) times—60 (66, 68, 72) sts. Cont until piece measures 11 (13, 14½, 16)" excluding border. **Shape neck:** Work across 20 (22, 22, 23) sts, join second ball of yarn and BO ctr 20 (22, 24, 26) sts, work across rem 20 (22,

22, 23) sts. Working both sides at same time, BO 3 sts at each neck edge once, dec 1 st at each neck edge EOR 5 (7, 7, 8) times. Work rem 12 sts for each side until piece measures 17 (19½, 21, 23)" excluding border. BO all sts.

front

Work as for back.

finishing

Sew shoulder and side seams. Beg at underarm seam, work *1 double crochet, chain 1; rep from * around each armhole. Beg at right shoulder seam, work *1 double crochet, chain 1; rep from * around neck edge.

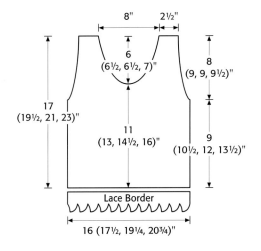

Fifi Tank

The adorable "frou-frou" collar and the sexy fit
is both contemporary and imaginative.

Skill Level: Intermediate

Sizes: Extra Small (Small, Medium, Large)

Finished Bust Measurements: 33 (36, 38½, 41)"

materials

- **A**   5 (6, 7, 8) skeins Berroco Pronto (50% cotton, 50% acrylic; 55 yds/skein), color 4451

- **B**   1 skein Trendsetter Dancer (57% polyester, 43% polyamid; 65 yds/skein), color 506

- Size 10½ needles (or size required to obtain gauge)

- Size 10 circular needle (24") for neck

GAUGE: 12 sts and 16 rows = 4" in St st with Pronto on size 10½ needles

---

melissa's point

If you like, single crochet along the neck edge and knit the frou-frou collar separately. That way, you can have twice the fun with two tanks in one. There are days for being more sedate.

 *skill builder*

Yᴀʀɴ Oᴠᴇʀ (YO) is what creates the hole or opening in a lace pattern. Wrap the yarn around the needle and go on to the next stitch. On the next row, the YO is worked as a stitch.

lace pattern

Row 1: K11 (13, 15, 17), YO, K2, SSK, K20, K2tog, K2, YO, K11 (13, 15, 17).

Row 2 and all even rows: Purl.

Row 3: K12 (14, 16, 18), YO, K2, SSK, K18, K2tog, K2, YO, K12 (14, 16, 18).

Row 5: K13 (15, 17, 19), YO, K2, SSK, K16, K2tog, K2, YO, K13 (15, 17, 19).

Row 7: K14 (16, 18, 20), YO, K2, SSK, K14, K2tog, K2, YO, K14 (16, 18, 20).

Row 9: K15 (17, 19, 21), YO, K2, SSK, K12, K2tog, K2, YO, K15 (17, 19, 21).

Row 11: K16 (18, 20, 22), YO, K2, SSK, K10, K2tog, K2, YO, K16 (18, 20, 22).

Row 13: K17 (19, 21, 23), YO, K2, SSK, K8, K2tog, K2, YO, K17 (19, 21, 23).

Row 15: K17 (19, 21, 23), K2tog, K2, YO, K8, YO, K2, SSK, K17 (19, 21, 23).

Row 17: K16 (18, 20, 22), K2tog, K2, YO, K10, YO, K2, SSK, K16 (18, 20, 22).

Row 19: K15 (17, 19, 21), K2tog, K2, YO, K12, YO, K2, SSK, K15 (17, 19, 21).

Row 21: K14 (16, 18, 20), K2tog, K2, YO, K14, YO, K2, SSK, K14 (16, 18, 20).

Row 23: K13 (15, 17, 19), K2tog, K2, YO, K16, YO, K2, SSK, K13 (15, 17, 19).

Row 25: K12 (14, 16, 18), K2tog, K2, YO, K18, YO, K2, SSK, K12 (14, 16, 18).

Row 27: K11 (13, 15, 17), K2tog, K2, YO, K20, YO, K2, SSK, K11 (13, 15, 17).

back

With size 10½ needles and A, CO 50 (54, 58, 62) sts. Work in St st until piece measures 10 (11, 12, 14½)". **Shape armholes**: BO 2 sts at beg of next 2 rows, dec 1 st at each edge EOR 6 times—34 (38, 42, 46) sts. Cont until piece measures 17 (18½, 19½, 22)". BO all sts.

front

Work as for back until piece measures 3 (4, 5, 6)". Work 27 rows of Lace patt. Work in St st until piece measures 10 (11, 12, 14½)". **Shape armholes**: BO 2 sts at beg of next 2 rows, dec 1 st at each edge EOR 6 times—34 (38, 42, 46) sts. Cont in St st until piece measures 14 (15½, 16½, 19)". **Shape neck**: Work across 11 (13, 15, 17) sts, join second ball of yarn and BO ctr 12 sts, work across rem 11 (13, 15, 17) sts. Working both sides at same time, dec 1 st at each neck edge EOR 3 (4, 4, 5) times—8 (9, 11, 12) sts. Cont until piece measures 17 (18½, 19½, 22)". BO all sts.

finishing

Sew shoulder seams. With size 10 circular needle and B, PU 60 sts evenly around neck edge and join (see page 15). Work 4" of garter st. Remember, when working in the round, that means *knit 1 row, purl 1 row; rep from *. BO all sts. Sew side seams.

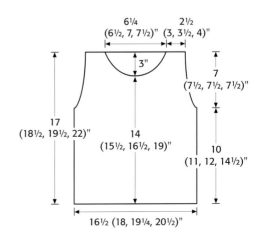

Draped Mock Neck Tank

Such an easy, effortless style—this is a flattering fit for all.

Skill Level: Beginner

Sizes: Petite (Extra Small, Small, Medium, Large, Extra Large)

Finished Bust Measurements: 33 (36, 38½, 41, 44, 46½)"

materials

- 7 (7, 8, 8, 9, 10) skeins Tahki Yarns Capri (100% Egyptian cotton; 52 yds/skein), color C03

- Size 13 needles (or size required to obtain gauge)

- Size 13 circular needle (16") for neck

- Stitch holder

GAUGE: 12 sts and 16 rows = 4" in St st

---

melissa's point

When knitting this tank, you will get to the shoulder shaping and think there is a typo. Just follow the pattern; the shaping will look weird, but the hard slant of the shoulder shaping provides the neck drape. Join the shoulder seams using V-to-V seaming.

 skill builder

$\mathcal{F}$OR A smoother edge, slip the first stitch whenever you start to bind off. This reduces the laddering effect and makes the seaming process easier.

V-TO-V SEAMING produces an invisible seam. Work from the right side, with the bound-off edges lined up stitch for stitch. Insert the yarn needle from the back to the front into the V of the stitch, just below the bound-off edge. *Insert the needle under two strands of the knit stitch on the second piece, then under the next two strands of the first piece, repeat from * to end of the bound-off edge. Carefully adjust the tension as you work, so the seam looks like the knitted work.

back

CO 50 (54, 58, 62, 66, 70) sts. Work in St st until piece measures 11 (12, 13, 14, 15, 15)". **Shape armholes:** BO 2 (2, 3, 4, 5, 6) sts at beg of next 2 rows. Work dec row [K3, K2tog, knit to last 5 sts, sl 1, K1, psso, K3] EOR 5 (5, 6, 6, 7, 8) times—36 (40, 40, 42, 42, 42) sts. Cont until piece measures 17½ (19, 20, 21½, 23, 23)". **Shape shoulders:** BO 1 st at beg of each row 12 (16, 16, 18, 18, 18) times. Place rem 24 sts on holder.

front

Work as for back.

finishing

Sew shoulder and side seams. With circular needle, knit rem neck sts from holder and work in St st for 1½". BO all sts. Fold neck in half toward the inside and tack in place.

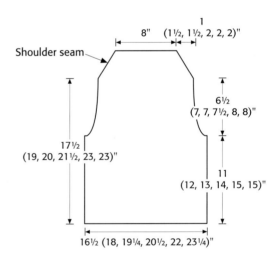

Ribbed Tank

This basically beautiful ribbed tank has a soft texture.
Wear it fitted for cocoon comfort, or block it for a soft, curved fit.

Skill Level: Beginner

Sizes: Small (Medium, Large)

Finished Bust Measurements: 34–37 (37½–40½, 41–44)"

materials

- **A**   5 (6, 7) skeins Muench String of Pearls (70% cotton, 20% viscose, 10% polyester; 99 yds/skein), color 4006

- **B**   5 (6, 7) skeins Crystal Palace Yarns Waikiki (70% rayon, 30% cotton; 105 yds/skein), color 2671

- Size 9 needles (or size required to obtain gauge)

- Size I crochet hook

GAUGE: 14 sts and 20 rows = 4" in K3, P3 Rib patt, slightly stretched, with 1 strand each of A and B held tog

---

melissa's point

Remember that ribbing pulls in quite a bit. Halfway through
the garment, you will think you are knitting for an eight-year-old.
Don't worry; it will be OK. The rib can give up to 3"
after it is blocked. By the way, Waikiki has a "Dry clean only" label,
but I've been washing it for years and it maintains its beauty.

EOR 4 (5, 5) times—38 (42, 48) sts. Cont in patt until piece measures 13 (14, 15)". **Shape neck**: Work across 12 (14, 16) sts, join second ball of yarn and BO ctr 14 (14, 16) sts, work across rem 12 (14, 16) sts. Working both sides at same time, BO 3 sts at each neck edge once, dec 1 st at each neck edge EOR 0 (2, 4) times. Work rem 9 sts on each side for strap until piece measures 18½ (21, 22)". BO all sts.

front

Work as for back. For a higher neck, as shown in green tank at right, beg neck shaping when piece measures 14 (15, 16).

finishing

Sew shoulder and side seams. Work 1 row of single crochet, followed by 1 row of shrimp stitch around neck and armhole edges (see page 15).

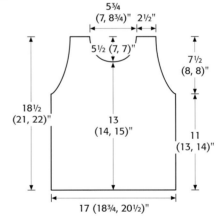

K3, P3 rib pattern (multiple of 6)

Row 1: *K3, P3; rep from * to end.

Row 2: Knit the knit sts and purl the purl sts.

Rep row 2.

back

With 1 strand of A and B held tog, CO 60 (66, 72) sts. Work in K3, P3 Rib patt until piece measures 11 (13, 14)". **Shape armholes**: BO 3 sts at beg of next 2 rows, BO 2 sts at beg of next 4 rows, dec 1 st at each edge

 skill builder

WHEN KNITTING, hold the yarn in back of the work. When purling, hold the yarn in front. Move yarn between the needles when changing between the knit and purl stitches.

Variations

Green Tank

- ◎ **A**   4 (5, 6) skeins Filatura Di Crosa Millefili Fine (100% cotton, 136 yds/skein), color 128

- ◎ **B**   5 (6, 7) skeins Crystal Palace Yarns Waikiki (70% rayon, 30% cotton; 105 yds/skein), color 2862

Beige Tank

- ◎ **A**   5 (6, 7) skeins Dale of Norway Svale (50% cotton, 40% viscose, 10% silk; 114 yds/skein), color 9425

- ◎ **B**   5 (6, 7) skeins Crystal Palace Yarns Waikiki (70% rayon, 30% cotton; 105 yds/skein), color 2862

Flora Tank

*A fabulously flowing draped neck and fantasy trim
highlight this figure-flattering style.*

Skill Level: Beginner

Sizes: Extra Small (Small, Medium, Large, Extra Large)

Finished Bust Measurements: 35 (38, 41, 43, 46)"

materials

- **A** 2 (3, 3, 3, 4) skeins Klaus Koch Kollektion Clipp (100% Egyptian cotton; 182 yds/skein), color 115

- **B** 1 skein Trendsetter Flora (77% polyester, 23% Tactel nylon; 94yds/skein), color 71

- Size 9 needles (or size required to obtain gauge)

- Size 9 circular needle (24") for neck

- Stitch holder

GAUGE: 16 sts and 20 rows = 4" in St st

---

melissa's point

When changing yarn, don't cut the first yarn. Tie on the
new yarn and when you need to return to the original yarn,
carry it loosely up the side edge. It won't be noticed
once the seam is complete and there will be
fewer ends to weave in.

 *skill builder*

To LENGTHEN OR SHORTEN THIS GARMENT, make adjustment to length after completing all rows of B but before armhole shaping.

back

With A, CO 70 (76, 82, 86, 92) sts. Work in St st for 2 rows. Change to B, work 8 rows. Change to A, work 4 rows. Change to B, work 4 rows. Change to A, work until piece measures 12 (13, 13, 14, 15)". **Shape armholes**: BO 4 sts at beg of next 2 rows, BO 3 sts at beg of next 2 rows, dec 1 st at each

 skill builder

W HEN MAKING the increase, M1, slant the stitch to the right on the beginning edge of your work and slant to the left for the second M1. It will provide a subtle slant to the stitch and gives your increases a clean look.

M1 right slant: On the knit side, insert the left needle from back to front under the horizontal ladder. Knit this lifted strand through the front to twist the stitch to the right.

Insert left needle from back to front under "running thread."

Knit into front of stitch.

M1 left slant: On the knit side, insert the left needle under the horizontal ladder. Knit this lifted strand through the back to twist the stitch to the left.

Insert left needle from front to back under "running thread."

Knit into back of stitch.

edge EOR 1 (1, 2, 3, 4) times—54 (60, 64, 66, 70) sts. Work until piece measures 19 (20, 20, 21½, 23)". BO rem sts.

front

Work as for back until armhole shaping is complete. **Shape neck**: On next RS row, work inc row as follows: K13 (14, 15, 16, 16) sts, M1, K28 (32, 34, 34, 38), M1, K13 (14, 15, 16, 16) sts. Work inc row EOR 5 more times, increasing center count by 2 sts each inc row. Work inc row every 4 rows 3 times—74 (80, 84, 86, 90) sts. Cont until piece measures 19 (20, 20, 21½, 23)". BO 11 (12, 13, 14, 16) sts at beg of next row, place ctr 52 (56, 58, 58, 58) sts on holder, BO rem 11 (12, 13, 14, 16) sts.

finishing

Sew shoulder seams. With circular needle, PU sts around neck and knit sts from holder (see page 15). Join ends and work in St st for 3". Remember, when working in the round, that means knit every row. BO all sts. Sew side seams.

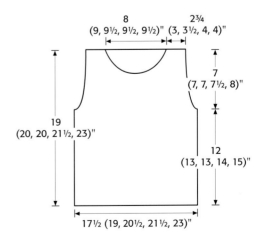

Twice As Nice Tank

This cabled tank is twice as nice when paired with the short Flair jacket without the crochet loops.

Skill Level: Intermediate

Sizes: Extra Small (Small, Medium, Large, and Extra Large)
Finished Bust Measurements: 34½ (36½, 38, 40, 42½)"

materials

- 5 (6, 7, 7, 8) skeins Trendsetter Yarns Marabella (50% polyamid, 50% Tactel nylon; 93 yds/skein), color 4207

- Size 8 needles (or size required to obtain gauge)

- Size 7 circular needle (24") for neck

- Cable needle

- Size F crochet hook

GAUGE: 18 sts and 22 rows = 4" in St st on size 8 needles

---

melissa's point
Make both the tank and jacket for a twin set.
You can then double up and wear them together or
pare down and wear them separately.

 *skill builder*

F OR A SLIGHTLY different look, reverse the twist of the cable. Hold the stitches on the cable needle in the back and the cables will then twist to the right.

cable left pattern (multiple of 12)

Rows: 1, 3, 5, 7, 11: P2, K8, P2.

Rows: 2, 4, 6, 8, 10: Knit the knit sts and purl the purl sts.

Row 9: P2, sl 4 sts to cn, hold in front, K4, K4 from cn, P2.

Row 12: Knit the knit sts and purl the purl sts.

Rep rows 1–12.

back

With size 8 needles, CO 78 (82, 86, 90, 96) sts. Work in St st patt until piece measures 11 (12, 13, 14, 14)". **Shape armholes:** BO 5 (5, 6, 6, 7) sts at beg of next 2 rows, dec 1 st at each edge EOR 6 (6, 6, 7, 7) times—56 (60, 62 , 64, 68) sts. Cont in patt until piece measures 18½ (19½, 21, 22, 23)". BO all sts.

front

With size 8 needles, CO 78 (82, 86, 90, 96) sts. Set up foundation row as follows: Knit across 33 (35, 37, 39, 42) sts, work Cable Left patt across ctr 12 sts, knit across rem 33 (35, 37, 39, 42) sts. Cont in patt until piece measures 11 (12, 13, 14, 14)". **Shape armholes:** BO 5 (5, 6, 6, 7) sts at beg of next 2 rows, dec 1 st at each edge EOR 6 (6, 6, 7, 7) times—56 (60, 62, 64, 68) sts. Cont in patt until piece measures 15½ (16½, 18, 19, 20)". **Shape neck:** Work in patt across 19 (21, 22, 23, 25) sts, join second ball of yarn and BO ctr 18 sts, work in patt across rem 19 (21, 22, 23, 25) sts. Working both sides at same time, BO 4 sts at each edge once, dec 1 st at each neck

edge EOR 4 times—11 (13, 14, 15, 17) sts for each shoulder. Cont in patt until piece measures 18½ (19½, 21, 22, 23)". BO rem sts for each shoulder.

finishing

Sew shoulder and side seams. With size 7 circular needle, PU sts evenly around neck edge (see page 15). Work in K1, P1 rib until neck measures 7". BO all sts in patt. Work 1 row of single crochet around armhole edges; then work 1 row of shrimp stitch (see page 15).

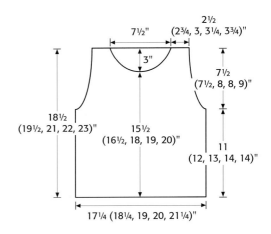

Terrific Tees

Seed Stitch Tee

*An elegant cobbled texture enhances a classic design
for a versatile and easy tee.*

Skill Level: Beginner

Sizes: Extra Small (Small, Medium, Large, Extra Large)

Finished Bust Measurements: 36 (38, 41, 44, 47)"

materials

- ◉ 5 (5, 6, 6, 7) skeins Karabella Yarns Softig (100% cotton;
  88 yds/skein), color 100

- ◉ Size 13 needles (or size required to obtain gauge)

- ◉ Size 10½ circular needle (24")

GAUGE: 11 sts and 16 rows = 4" in Seed Stitch patt on size 13 needles

---

melissa's point

I know seed stitch can be such a pain,
but at this gauge, it's a snap. Voilà—instant gratification.

 *skill builder*

SEED STITCH gives a very firm stitch that does not roll. The edge remains crisp without any additional edging.

seed stitch pattern

Row 1: K1, P1.

Row 2: Purl the knit sts and knit the purl sts.

Rep row 2.

back

With size 13 needles, CO 49 (53, 57, 61, 65) sts. Work in seed st until piece measures 11 (12, 13, 14, 15)". **Shape armholes**: BO 3 sts at beg of next 2 rows, dec 1 st at each edge EOR 5 (5, 7, 7, 9) times—33 (37, 37, 41, 41) sts. Cont in seed st until piece measures 19 (20, 21, 22, 23)". BO all sts in patt.

front

Work as for back until piece measures 16 (17, 18, 19, 20)". **Shape neck**: Work in patt across 10 (12, 12, 14, 14) sts, join second ball of yarn and BO ctr 13 sts, work in patt across rem 10 (12, 12, 14, 14) sts. Working both sides at same time, dec 1 st at each neck edge EOR twice. When piece measures 19 (20, 21, 22, 23)", BO 8 (10, 10, 12, 12) sts in patt for each shoulder.

sleeves

With size 13 needles, CO 37 (39, 41, 41, 43) sts. Work in seed st for 3". **Shape cap**: BO 3 sts at beg of next 2 rows, dec 1 st at each edge EOR 10 times, BO 2 sts at beg of next 2 rows. BO rem sts in patt.

finishing

Sew shoulder seams. With size 10½ circular needle, PU sts evenly around neck edge (see page 15). Work in seed st for 4". BO all sts in patt. Sew sleeve and side seams.

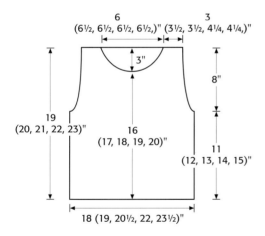

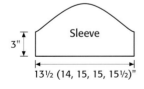

Between the Lines Tee

The striking vertical lines provide a refined slimming look.

Skill Level: Beginner

Sizes: Extra Small (Small, Medium, Large, Extra Large)

Finished Bust Measurements: 36 (38, 40½, 43, 45)"

materials

- 10 (11, 12, 13, 14) skeins Berroco Seta (60% silk, 40% rayon; 51 yds/skein), color 4157

- Size 10½ needles (or size required to obtain gauge)

- Size 10 circular needle (24") for neck

- 2 stitch holders

GAUGE: 14 sts and 20 rows = 4" in patt st on size 10½ needles

---

melissa's point
Most knitters would rather knit
than purl and that seems to give purls
a bad rap. Here the purls accent the knit stitches,
creating the long, slimming lines.

skill builder

For a very different look, use the reverse side as the right side (see detail photo at bottom left of facing page). Simply sew together with the reverse side on the outside and tuck the ends in the back.

pattern stitch (multiple of 4 + 3)

Row 1 (WS): K3, *P1, K3*; rep from * to end.

Row 2 (RS): P3, *K1, P3*; rep from * to end.

Rep rows 1 and 2.

back

With size 10½ needles, CO 63 (67, 71, 75, 79) sts. Work in patt st until piece measures 13 (13, 14, 14, 15)". **Shape armholes:** BO 4 sts at beg of next 2 rows, dec 1 st at each edge EOR 6 (7, 8, 8, 9) times—43 (45, 47, 51, 53) sts. Cont in patt until piece measures 22 (22, 23, 23, 24)". BO 12 sts at beg of next 2 rows. Place 19 (21, 23, 27, 29) sts on holder.

front

Work as for back until piece measures 19 (19, 20, 20, 21)". **Shape neck:** Work in patt across 13 (14, 15, 16, 17) sts, place ctr 17 (17, 17, 19, 19) sts on holder, join second ball of yarn and work in patt across rem 13 (14, 15, 16,

17) sts. Working both sides at same time, dec 1 st at each neck edge EOR 1 (2, 3, 4, 5) times. Work until piece measures 22 (22, 23, 23, 24)". BO 12 sts in patt for each shoulder.

sleeves

With size 10½ needles, CO 43 (47, 51, 53, 53) sts. Work in patt st until piece measures 4". **Shape cap:** BO 3 sts at beg of next 2 rows, dec 1 st at each edge EOR 12 times, BO 2 sts at beg of next 2 (4, 4, 4, 4) rows. BO rem sts in patt.

finishing

Sew shoulder seams. **Neckband:** With size 10 circular needle, work in patt all back sts from holder, PU 15 (13, 15, 13, 15) sts along side, work in patt all front sts from holder, PU 15 (13, 15, 13, 15) sts along side—46 (46, 50, 52, 56) sts. Work in patt for 2". BO all sts in patt. Sew sleeve and side seams.

Detail of the Reverse Side of the Sweater
(See Skill Builder)

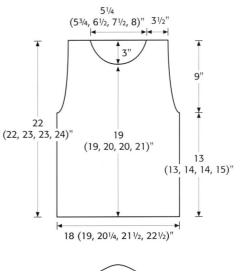

Butterfly Tee

A dramatic pattern adorns a comfortable style.
It's sure to become your favorite tee.

Skill Level: Intermediate

Sizes: Small (Medium, Large, Extra Large)

Finished Bust Measurements: 35 (40, 44, 48)"

materials

⊚ 4 (4, 5, 5) skeins Klaus Koch Kollektion Clipp (100% Egyptian cotton; 182 yds/skein), color 5

⊚ Size 8 needles (or size required to obtain gauge)

⊚ Size 7 needles

⊚ Size 7 circular needle (24") for neck

GAUGE: 18 sts and 24 rows = 4" in Pattern A on size 8 needles

melissa's point
What an enjoyable piece to make!
Don't let the pattern scare you; take it row by row. It's as easy
as painting by number. Try it; you'll be pleasantly surprised.

the 5 strands with next st tog as 1 st, P9; rep from *, end P4.

Rows 11, 13, 15, 17, and 19: K7, *sl 5 wyif, K5; rep from *, end sl 5 wyif, K7.

Rows 12, 14, 16, and 18: Purl.

Row 20: P9, *insert needle down through 5 loose strands, bring them up and purl them tog with next st as before, P9; rep from * to end.

Rep rows 1–20.

pattern B (multiple of 6 + 7 [5, 9, 7])

Row 1: K1 (0, 2, 1) sts, *K5, K1 (wrap twice); rep from *, end K6 (5, 7, 6) sts.

Row 2: P1 (0, 2, 1) sts, *P5, P1 (drop wrap); rep from *, end P6 (5, 7, 6) sts.

Rows 3 and 5: K1 (0, 2, 1) sts, *K5, sl 1 wyib; rep from *, end K6 (5, 7, 6) sts.

Rows 4 and 6: P1 (0, 2, 1) sts, *P5, sl 1 wyif; rep from *, end P6 (5, 7, 6) sts.

Row 7: K3 (2, 4, 3) sts, K1 (wrap twice), *K5, K1 (wrap twice); rep from *, end K3 (2, 4, 3) sts.

Row 8: P3 (2, 4, 3) sts, P1 (drop wrap), *P5, P1 (drop wrap); rep from *, end P3 (2, 4, 3) sts.

Rows 9 and 11: K3 (2, 4, 3) sts, sl 1 wyib, *K5, sl 1 wyib; rep from *, end K3 (2, 4, 3) sts.

Rows 10 and 12: P3 (2, 4, 3) sts, sl 1 wyif, *P5, sl 1 wyif; rep from *, end P3 (2, 4, 3) sts.

Rep rows 1–12.

skill builder

Slipping stitches with the yarn in front creates a bar across the slipped stitches. It is this bar that is then gathered up to form the butterfly.

pattern A (multiple of 10 + 9)

Rows 1, 3, 5, 7, and 9 (RS): K2, *sl 5 wyif, K5, rep from *, end sl 5 wyif, K2.

Rows 2, 4, 6, and 8: Purl.

Row 10: P4; *on next stitch (which is ctr st of slipped group), insert right needle down through the 5 loose strands, bring needle up and transfer the 5 strands to left needle, purl

back

With size 7 needles, CO 79 (89, 99, 109) sts. Work in garter st for 6 rows. Change to size 8 needles, beg Pattern A, and work for 40 (40, 60, 60) rows, completing 4 (4, 6, 6) rows of butterflies. Beg Pattern B and work until piece measures 18 (19, 20, 21)". BO all sts.

front

Work as for back until piece measures 15 (16, 17, 18)". **Shape neck:** Work in patt across 31 (36, 41, 46) sts, join second ball of yarn and BO ctr 17 sts, work in patt across rem 31 (36, 41, 46) sts. Working both sides at same time, BO 4 sts at each neck edge once, BO 3 sts at each neck edge once, BO 2 sts at each neck edge once, dec 1 st at each neck edge once. Work until piece measures 18 (19, 20, 21)". BO 21 (26, 31, 36) sts for each shoulder.

sleeves

With size 7 needles, CO 69 (69, 79, 79) sts. Work in garter st for 6 rows. Change to size 8 needles and work in Pattern A, completing rows 1–20 once. Work in St st for 2 rows. BO all sts.

finishing

Sew shoulder seams. **Neckband:** With size 7 circular needle, PU sts around neck edge (see page 15) and work in garter st for 6 rows. Remember, when working in the round, that means knit 1 row, purl 1 row. BO all sts.

Sew sleeve and side seams.

Variation

4 (4, 5, 5) skeins Schafer Yarns Helene (50% silk, 50% wool; 218 yds/skein), hand painted. Sleeves were made longer by completing an additional 20 rows of butterfly pattern.

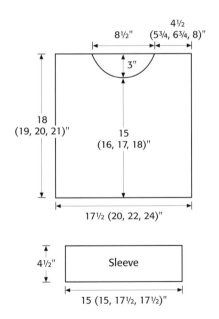

Hanging Out Tee

This distinctive top with a cap sleeve will dangle and delight!

Skill Level: Intermediate

Sizes: Extra Small (Small, Medium, Large, Extra Large)

Finished measurements: 32 (34, 36½, 39, 44½)"

materials

- 8 (10, 10, 11, 12) balls Trendsetter Binario (100% polyamid; 82 yds/ball) color 101

- Size 10 needles (or size required to obtain gauge)

GAUGE: 13.5 sts and 18 rows = 4" in St st
with 2 strands of yarn held tog

---

melissa's point

Don't let all the cut-and-ties scare you;
they consume about as much time as cabling every six rows.
So cut loose!

 skill builder

Using the first half of a square knot, firmly tie the yarn around the 4" cut tail. Then slip the half knot up to the stitch on the needle.

hanging pattern (multiple of 9)

Rows 1, 3, 7, and 9: Knit.

Rows 2, 4, 6, 8, and 10: Purl.

Row 5: *K9, leave 4" tail, cut yarn. Leave 4" tail, tie on, rep from *, end K9 (4, 8, 3, 4).

Row 11: *K4, leave 4" tail, cut yarn. Leave 4" tail, tie on, K5, rep from *, end K0 (4, 8, 3, 4).

Row 12: Purl.

Rep rows 1–12.

back

With 2 strands of yarn held tog, CO 54 (58, 62, 66, 76) sts, work in hanging patt until piece measures 11". **Shape sleeves:** Maintain est patt, inc 1 st at each edge EOR 4 (5, 6, 6, 7) times—62 (68, 74, 78, 90) sts. Cast on 4 sts at each edge once—70 (76, 82, 86, 98) sts. Cont in patt until piece measures 16 (17, 17½, 18, 18)". **Shape neck:** Work across 27 (30, 33, 35, 41) sts, join a second ball of yarn and BO ctr 16 sts, work across rem 27 (30, 33, 35, 41) sts. Working both sides at same

time, BO 2 sts at each neck edge once, dec 1 st at each neck edge EOR 4 times—21 (24, 27, 29, 35) sts. Cont in patt until piece measures 17 (18, 18½, 19, 19)". **Shape shoulders:** BO 4 (5, 6, 7, 8) sts at side edge 2 times. BO 13 (14, 15, 15, 19) sts at each shoulder.

front

Work as for back.

finishing

Sew shoulder and side seams.

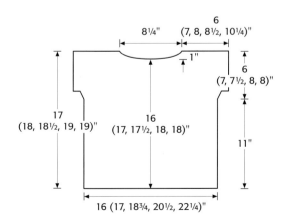

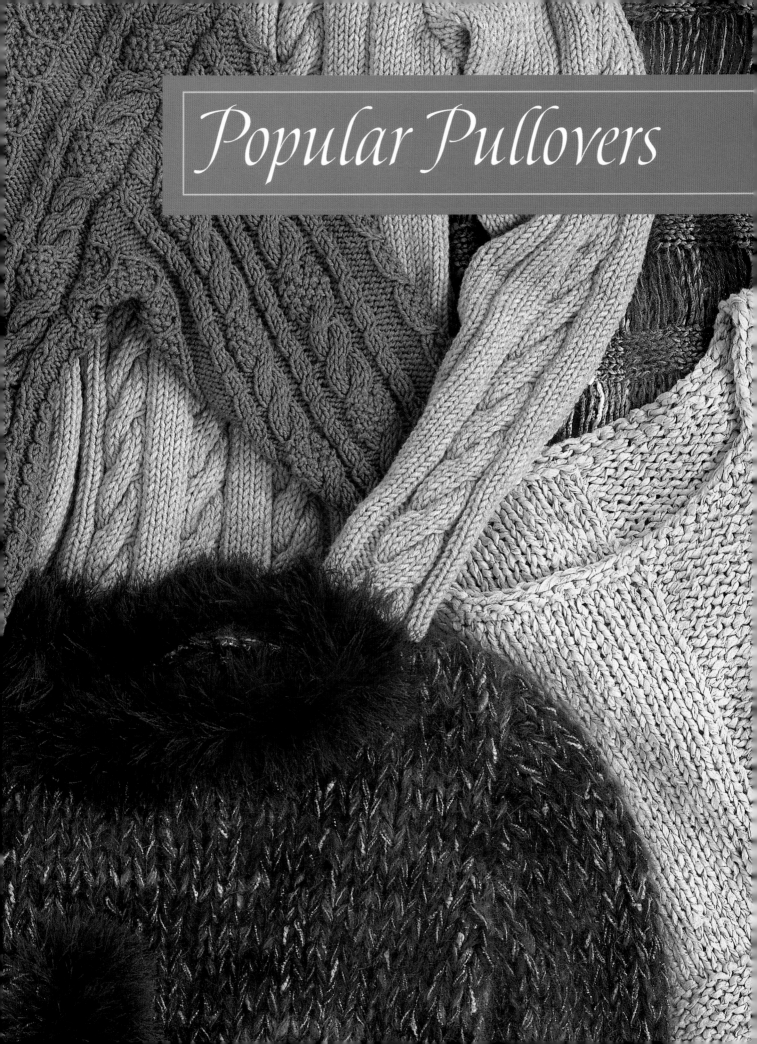

Popular Pullovers

Garden of Cables Pullover

Wander down the primrose path in this garden.
Perfectly designed cables give incredible lines.

Skill Level: Intermediate

Sizes: Small/Medium (Large, Extra Large)

Finished Bust Measurements: 48 (50, 54)"

materials

- 12 (13, 13) skeins Filatura di Crosa Zara (100% wool; 136 yds/skein), color 1661

- Size 8 needles (or size required to obtain gauge)

- Size 6 needles

- Cable needle

GAUGE: 21 sts and 25 rows = 4" in C8S patt,
slightly stretched, on size 8 needles

---

melissa's point

For those of you who are visual learners, don't let all the words intimidate you. After the cable rib, the two increase stitches become the C8S panel. The K2, P2, K2 forms the C6 panel.

skill builder

WHEN WORKING in a rib pattern, bind off in pattern. This means knit the knit stitches and purl the purl stitches as you bind off.

C2 for cable rib (multiple of 2)

Row 1: Sl 1 st to cn, hold in front, K1, K1 from cn.

Row 2: Purl.

Row 3: Knit.

Row 4: Purl.

Rep rows 1–4.

C6 (multiple of 6)

Row 1: Sl 3 sts to cn, hold in back, K3, K3 from cn.

Rows 2, 4, 6, and 8: Purl.

Rows 3, 5, and 7: Knit.

Rows 9-16: Rep rows 1–8 once more.

Rows 17 and 18: Rep rows 1 and 2.

Rows 19-24: Work seed st for 6 rows.

Rep these 24 rows.

seed stitch (multiple of 6)

Row 1: K1, P1, K1, P1, K1, P1.

Row 2: Knit the purl sts and purl the knit sts.

Rep row 2.

C8S (multiple of 8)

Row 1: Sl 3 sts to cn, hold in back, K1, work 3 sts in seed st from cn, sl 1 st to cn, hold in front, work 3 sts in seed st, K1 from cn.

Rows 2, 4, and 6: P1, work 6 sts in seed st, P1.

Rows 3, 5, and 7: K1, work 6 sts in seed st, K1.

Row 8: P1, work 6 sts in seed st, P1.

Rep rows 1–8.

back

With size 6 needles, CO 126 (134, 142) sts. Establish Cable Rib as follows:

Small/Medium (RS): P2, C2, P2, K2, P2, K2, P2, C2, P2, K2, P2, C2, P2, K2, P2, C2, P2, K2, P2, K2, P2, C2, P2, K2, P2, K2, P2, C2, P2, K2, P2, C2 (completed ctr 2 sts), work patt in reverse to complete row, beg with P2.

Large (RS): P2, K2, P2, C2, P2, K2, P2, K2, P2, C2, P2, K2, P2, C2, P2, K2, P2, C2, P2, K2, P2, K2, P2, C2, P2, K2, P2, K2, P2, C2, P2, K2, P2, C2 (completed ctr 2 sts), work patt in reverse to complete row, beg with P2.

Extra Large (RS): P6, K2, P2, C2, P2, K2, P2, K2, P2, C2, P2, K2, P2, C2, P2, K2, P2, C2, P2, K2, P2, K2, P2, C2, P2, K2, P2, K2, P2, C2, P2, K2, P2, C2 (completed ctr 2 sts), work patt in reverse to complete row, beg with P2.

Work in patt for 2½", ending on RS row. Inc row (WS): Work in est patt 22 (26, 30) sts, M1, work 1 st, M1, work 1 st, work 38 stitches, [M1, work 1 st, M1, work 1 st (ctr 4 sts)], work patt in reverse to complete row—132 (140, 148) sts.

Change to size 8 needles. Set up next RS row as follows:

Small/Medium (RS): P2, C2, P2, C6, P2, C2, P4, C8S, P4, C2, P2, C6, P2, C2, P2, C6, P2, C2, P4, C8S (ctr 8 sts), work patt in reverse to complete row, beg with P4.

Large (RS): P2, C2, P2, C2, P2, C6, P2, C2, P4, C8S, P4, C2, P2, C6, P2, C2, P2, C6, P2, C2, P4, C8S (ctr 8 sts), work patt in reverse to complete row, beg with P4.

Extra Large (RS): P6, C2, P2, C2, P2, C6, P2, C2, P4, C8S, P4, C2, P2, C6, P2, C2, P2, C6, P2, C2, P4, C8S (ctr 8 sts), work patt in reverse to complete row, beg with P4.

Cont in patt until piece measures 10½ (13½, 15½)". **Shape armholes:** BO 5 (7, 7) sts at beg of next 2 rows—122 (126, 134) sts. Cont in patt until piece measures 18" (21, 23)". **Shape neck:** Work in patt across 51 (53, 57) sts, join second ball of yarn and BO ctr 20 sts, work in patt across rem 51 (53, 57) sts. Working both sides at same time, BO 3 sts at each neck edge once, BO 2 sts at each neck edge once, dec 1 st at each neck edge EOR 3 times. Cont in patt until piece measures 20 (23, 25)". BO 43 (45, 49) sts in patt for each shoulder.

front

Work as for back until piece measures 17 (20, 22)". Shape neck as for back. Cont in patt until piece measures 20 (23, 25)". BO rem sts in patt.

sleeves

With size 6 needles, CO 54 (54, 62) sts. Establish Cable Rib as follows:

Small/Medium and Large: P2, K2, P2, C2, P2, K2, P2, K2, P2, C2, P2, K2, P2, C2 (ctr 2 sts), work patt in reverse to complete row, beg with P2.

Extra Large: P2, K2, P2, K2, P2, C2, P2, K2, P2, K2, P2, C2, P2, K2, P2, C2 (ctr 2 sts), work patt in reverse to complete row, beg with P2.

Work in est patt for 7", end on RS row.

Inc row (WS): Work 26 (26, 30) sts, [M1, work 1 st, M1, work 1 st (ctr 4 sts)], work patt in reverse to complete row—56 (56, 64) sts.

Change to size 8 needles, set up next RS row as follows:

Small/Medium and Large: P2, C2, P2, C2, P2, C6, P2, C2, P4, C8S (ctr 8 sts), work patt in reverse to complete row, beg with P4.

Extra Large: P2, C6, P2, C2, P2, C6, P2, C2, P4, C8S (ctr 8 sts), work patt in reverse to complete row, beg with P4.

Work in patt, inc 1 st at each edge every 2 rows 23 times—102 (102, 110) sts. Cont in patt until piece measures 17" or desired length. **Shape cap**: BO 8 sts at beg of next 6 rows. BO rem sts in patt.

finishing

Sew shoulder seams. With size 6 needles, PU (126 (134, 142) sts around neck edge and set up Cable Rib as for back. Work in patt for 3". BO. Fold toward the inside and tack in place. Sew sleeve and side seams.

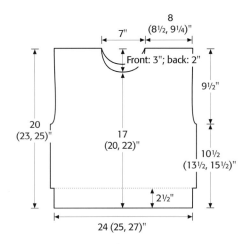

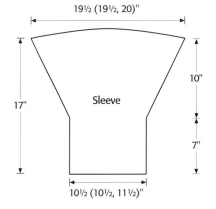

Drop Two Pullover

The dropped stitches give this sweater its name. It is the essence of exquisite simplicity and artfulness. Wear over a camisole or black silk dress.

Skill Level: Intermediate

Sizes: Small (Medium, Large)

Finished Bust Measurements: 40 (43, 46)"

materials

◉ **A**   2 skeins S. Charles Venus (95% viscose, 5% polyamid; 83 yds/skein), color 6

◉ **B**   2 (2, 3) skeins S. Charles Ritratto (28% mohair, 53% viscose, 10% polamide, 9% polyester; 198 yds/skein), color 6 worked double

◉ **C**   2 skeins S. Charles Venus, color 3

◉ **D**   1 skein S. Charles Venus, color 1

◉ **E**   1 (1, 2) skeins S. Charles Ritratto, color 42 worked double

◉ **F**   1 (1, 2) skeins S. Charles Ritratto, color 10 worked double

◉ Size 9 needles (or size required to obtain gauge)

GAUGE: 16 sts and 20 rows = 4" in St st, with double strand of Ritratto

---

melissa's point
Please, wait to put your jewelry on until after you have
this sweater on. You don't want to snag the threads.

color stripe pattern

Stripe 1: 4 rows of A

Stripe 2: 6 rows of B

Stripe 3: 4 rows of C

Stripe 4: 1 row of D

Stripe 5: 4 rows of C

Stripe 6: 5 rows of E

Stripe 7: 3 rows of B

Stripe 8: 4 rows of A

Stripe 9: 5 rows of F

Rep 1–9 for stripe patt.

back

CO 46 (52, 58) sts and work in St st.

Small: Beg with stripe 1, work 3 complete color-stripe-pattern repeats.

Medium: Beg with stripe 7, work 3 complete color patt repeats, end with stripes 7–9.

Large: Beg with stripe 4, work 3 complete color patt repeats, end with stripes 4–9.

BO row: *BO 4 sts, drop 2 sts, rep from * across to last 4 sts, BO rem sts. Let the dropped sts run completely to the opposite edge.

> ═══ **melissa's point** ═══
> The side-to-side construction of this sweater means the cast-on
> and bind-off edges become the side seams.

front

Work as for back.

sleeves

Beg with stripe 1 and follow color patt rep. *CO 5 sts, work 2 rows in St st, rep from * until there are 40 sts on needle. Work in stripe patt until larger edge (shoulder edge) measures 16 (18, 20)". **On next knit row, BO 4 sts, drop 2 sts, BO 1 st, knit to end of row. Next row: Purl. Rep from ** until 3 sts rem. BO rem sts.

finishing

Sew 5" shoulder seams. Sew sleeve and side seams.

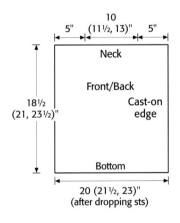

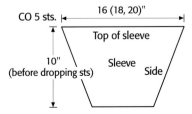

DROPPING THE stitches creates the laddering effect and will dramatically elongate the knit piece. Be sure to let the dropped stitches run to the opposite cast-on edge. The bind-off stitches over the dropped stitches should be loose enough to accommodate the length of the ladders.

1. Bind off normally up to the stitches to be dropped. Make the bind-off loop on the right needle large. Drop two stitches and let them unravel.

2. Unravel the two stitches to the cast-on edge. Adjust the bind-off loop to span the distance to the next stitch over the dropped stitches.

3. Complete the bind-off over the dropped stitches.

4. Bind off normally. The area where the stitches were dropped should not be pulled or puckered and the laddering should be even.

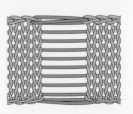

Classic Cable Pullover

This classic is dramatically sculptured
for a personal fashion statement.

Skill Level: Intermediate

Sizes: Extra Small (Small, Medium, Large, Extra Large)

Finished Bust Measurements: 35 (41, 46, 50, 55)"

materials

◉ 11 (12, 14, 16, 18) skeins Filatura di Crosa Luna (100% virgin wool; 88 yds/skein), color 1

◉ Size 9 needles (or size required to obtain gauge)

◉ Cable needle

◉ Stitch holder

GAUGE: 16 sts and 20 rows = 4" in St st

---

melissa's point

This piece works great with either
cotton or wool. Make it without the sleeves
and you'll have a chic tank.

*T*O COUNT the rows between the cable crosses, sweep your finger on the back side of the previous cable twist to find the hole at the point of the last cross. Count the rows from this point. When binding off, knit two stitches together over the cable stitches.

cable pattern (multiple of 8)

Rows 1, 3, and 5 (RS): K8.

Rows 2, 4, and 6 (WS): Purl.

Row 7: Sl 4 sts to cn, hold in front, K4, K4 from cn.

Row 8: Purl.

Rep rows 1–8.

K2, P2 rib pattern (multiple of 4)

Row 1: K2, P2.

Row 2: Knit the knit sts and purl the purl sts.
Rep row 2.

back

CO 70 (82, 92, 100, 110) sts. Set up foundation row as follows:

P2, K0 (3, 8, 12, 17), P0 (3, 3, 3, 3), K6, P3. Work Cable patt, P3, K6, P3, work Cable patt, P3, K6, P3, work Cable patt, P3, K6, P2 (3, 3, 3, 3), K0 (3, 8, 12, 17), P0 (2, 2, 2, 2).

Work in patt until piece measures 11½ (13½, 14, 15, 16)". **Shape armholes**: BO 3 sts at beg of next 2 rows, dec 1 st at each edge EOR 4 times—56 (68, 78, 86, 96) sts. Cont in patt until piece measures 19 (21, 22, 23, 24½)". BO rem sts in patt.

front

Work as for back until piece measures 16 (18, 19, 20, 21½)". **Shape neck**: Work in patt across 20 (26, 30, 34, 38) sts, join second ball of yarn and place ctr 16 (16, 18, 18, 20) sts on holder, work in patt across rem 20 (26, 30, 34, 38) sts. Working both sides at same time, BO 3 sts at each neck edge once, dec 1 st at each neck edge EOR 3 times. Cont in patt until piece measures 19 (21, 22, 23, 24½)". BO 14 (20, 24, 28, 32) sts in patt for each shoulder.

sleeves

CO 40 sts. Set up foundation row as follows:

P2, K2, P3, K6, P3, work Cable patt, P3, K6, P3, K2, P2.

Work in est patt for 2"; then inc 1 st at each edge every 4 rows 16 (16, 17, 17, 18) times— 72 (72, 74, 74, 76) sts. For better seams, work inc 2 sts from each edge. Cont in patt until piece measures 16 (16, 16, 17, 17)" or desired length. **Shape cap**: BO 4 sts at beg of next 2 rows, BO 2 sts at beg of next 2 rows, dec 1 st at each edge EOR 10 times. BO rem sts in patt. When working BO over cable sts, K2tog as you BO across the 8 cable sts.

finishing

Sew shoulder seams. PU 30 sts across back, PU 16 sts along side, work ctr sts in patt from holder, PU 16 sts along side—78 (78, 80, 80, 82) sts. Work in K2, P2 rib and cont ctr cable for 4". BO rem sts. Sew sleeve and side seams.

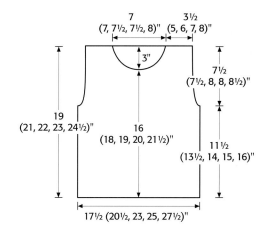

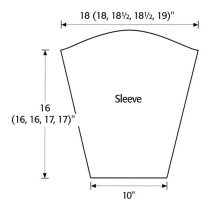

Rib Turtleneck Pullover

This pullover is sleek and snug for an absolute fit.

Skill Level: Beginner

Sizes: Extra Small (Small, Medium, Large, Extra Large)

Finished Bust Measurements: 33 (35, 39½, 43½, 46)"

materials

- ◎ **A** 7 (8, 9, 10, 11) skeins Filatura di Crosa Luna (100% virgin wool; 88 yds/skein), color 2
- ◎ **B** 7 (8, 9, 10, 11) skeins Filatura di Crosa Luna, color 01
- ◎ Size 10½ needles (or size required to obtain gauge)
- ◎ Size 10½ circular needle (24") for neck
- ◎ Stitch holder

GAUGE: 15 sts and 16 rows = 4" in K2, P2 Rib patt, slightly stretched, with 1 strand each of A and B held tog

---

melissa's point

This sweater is like a favorite pair of shoes;
I'll take one in every color.

 *skill builder*

*C*HECK YOUR gauge over the ribbed pattern by stretching the fabric only as much as you want the fabric to stretch when wearing the garment. Pin in position before measuring gauge.

K2, P2 rib pattern (multiple of 4)

Row 1: K2, P2.

Row 2: Knit the knit sts and purl the purl sts.

Rep row 2.

back

With 1 strand of A and B held tog, CO 56 (60, 68, 76, 80) sts. Work in K2, P2 Rib patt for 3". Cont in patt, inc 1 st at each edge every 6 rows 3 times—62 (66, 74, 82, 86) sts. Cont in patt until piece measures 12 (13, 14, 15, 15)". **Shape armholes:** BO 4 sts at beg of next 2 rows, dec 1 st at each edge EOR 2 (2, 3, 4, 5) times—50 (54, 60, 66, 68) sts. Cont in patt until piece measures 20 (21, 22, 23, 23)". BO rem sts in patt.

front

Work as for back until piece measures 17 (18, 19, 20, 20)". **Shape neck:** Work in patt across 20 (22, 25, 28, 29) sts, join second ball of yarn and place ctr 10 sts on holder, work in patt across rem 20 (22, 25, 28, 29) sts. Working both sides at same time, BO 3 sts at each neck edge once, BO 2 sts at each neck edge once, dec 1 st at each neck edge once. Cont in patt until piece measures 20 (21, 22, 23, 23)". BO 14 (16, 19, 22, 23) sts in patt for each shoulder.

sleeves

With 1 strand of A and B held tog, CO 28 (28, 32, 36, 36) sts. Work in K2, P2 Rib patt, inc 1 st at each edge every 6 rows 12 (13, 14, 16, 18) times—52 (54, 60, 68, 72) sts. For better seams, work inc 2 sts from each edge. Cont in patt until piece measures 15½ (16, 16, 16½,

16½)" or desired length. **Shape cap:** BO 4 sts at beg of next 2 rows, BO 2 sts at beg of next 2 rows 0 (0, 0, 1, 1) time, dec 1 st at each edge EOR 14 (15, 18, 19, 21) times, BO 3 sts at beg of next 4 rows. BO rem sts in patt.

finishing

Sew shoulder seams. With circular needle, PU a total of 64 (64, 68, 68, 68) sts (including 10 sts on holder) around neck edge and work K2, P2 Rib patt for 3½". BO in patt. Sew sleeve and side seams.

Variation

See inset photo on facing page.

9 (10, 12, 13, 14) skeins Prism Yarn Matisse (50% wool, 50% polyester, 70 yds/skein), color Alpine. Yarn worked single throughout.

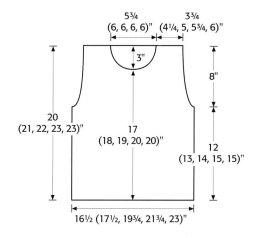

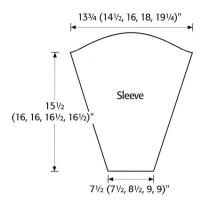

Pompom Pullover

Light and lofty, this sweater is the epitome of texture.

Skill Level: Beginner

Sizes: Extra Small (Small, Medium, Large, Extra Large)

Finished Bust Measurements: 37 (39, 41, 45, 47)"

materials

- **A**   7 (8, 9, 10, 11) skeins Filatura di Crosa Pom Pom (85% wool, 15% acrylic; 60 yds/skein), color 1100
- **B**   6 (7, 8, 9, 10) skeins Filatura di Crosa Pom Pom, color 105
- Size 15 needles (or size required to obtain gauge)
- Size 15 circular needle (24") for neck

GAUGE: 7.4 sts and 12 rows = 4" in St st with 2 strands of yarn held tog

---

melissa's point

Six or eight hours and you're done.
It's perfect for the weekend. Put down the size 6 needle project
and give yourself a treat. Knit it a bit longer if you have to
cover those love handles.

 skill builder

THE NUBBY TEXTURE of the PomPom yarn is not suitable for sewing the pieces together. Use a smooth, thinner yarn of similar color to sew seams. Pull the yarn securely while sewing but not tight enough to cause puckers.

stockinette stitch

Row 1: Knit.

Row 2: Purl.

Rep rows 1 and 2.

reverse stockinette stitch

Row 1: Purl.

Row 2: Knit.

Rep rows 1 and 2.

back

With 1 strand of A and B held tog, CO 34 (36, 38, 42, 44) sts. Work in St st until piece measures 12 (13, 13, 13, 14)". **Shape armholes**: BO 2 sts at beg of next 2 rows, dec 1 st at each end EOR 3 times—24 (26, 28, 32, 34) sts. Cont in St st until piece measures 19 (20, 21, 21, 22)". BO rem sts.

front

Work as for back until piece measures 16 (17, 18, 18, 19)". **Shape neck**: Work across 8 (9, 10, 12, 13) sts, join second ball of yarn and BO ctr 8 sts, work across rem 8 (9, 10, 12, 13) sts. Working both sides at same time, dec 1 st at each neck edge EOR 2 times. Cont until piece measures 19 (20, 21, 21, 22)". BO 6 (7, 8, 10, 11) sts for each shoulder.

sleeves

With 2 strands of A held tog, CO 20 (20, 22, 22, 24) sts. Work 8 rows in St st. Change to 1 strand of A and B held tog, work rev St st, inc 1 st at each edge every 6 rows 6 times— 32 (32, 34, 34, 36) sts. For better seams, work inc 2 sts from each edge. Cont until piece measures 16½" or desired length. **Shape cap**: BO 2 sts at beg of next 2 rows, dec 1 st at each end EOR 6 times, BO 2 sts at beg of next 3 rows. BO rem sts.

finishing

Sew shoulder seams. With circular needle and 2 strands of A held tog, PU 32 sts around neck edge and work in St st for 1½". BO all sts. Sew sleeve and side seams.

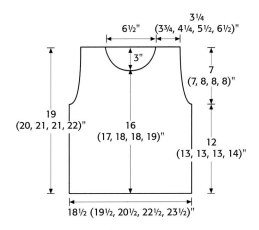

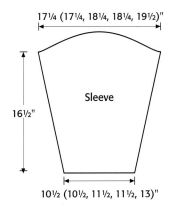

Four Corners Pullover

Whatever your angle, you'll be right with this versatile pullover.

Skill Level: Beginner

Sizes: Small (Medium, Large, Extra Large)

Finished Bust Measurements: 36 (39, 43½, 46½)"

materials

⊚ 15 (16, 17, 18) skeins Filatura Di Crosa Ibisco (80% acrylic, 20% polyamid; 41 yds/skein), color 101

⊚ Size 13 needles (or size required to obtain gauge)

⊚ Size I crochet hook

GAUGE: 11 sts and 16 rows = 4" in St st on size 13 needles

melissa's point

This pullover is so adaptable, it can be worn as
a beach cover-up or over dressy slacks with pearls
for an evening out.

 *skill builder*

$\mathcal{S}$INGLE CROCHET (sc): Working from the right to left, insert hook into the stitch, YO, pull through (2 loops on hook). YO and pull through both loops on hook.

pattern A

Row 1: K25 (27, 30, 32) sts, P25 (27, 30, 32) sts.

Row 2: Knit the knit sts and purl the purl sts.

Rep row 2.

pattern B

Row 1: P25 (27, 30, 32) sts, K25 (27, 30, 32) sts.

Row 2: Knit the knit sts and purl the purl sts.

Rep row 2.

back

With size 13 needles, CO 50 (54, 60, 64) sts. Work in Patt A until piece measures 11 (12, 13, 14)". Work in Patt B until piece measures 20 (21, 25, 26)". BO all sts loosely.

front

Work as for back until piece measures 17 (18, 22, 23)". **Shape neck**: Work across 18 (20, 23, 25) sts, join a second ball of yarn and BO ctr 14 sts, work across rem 18 (20, 23, 25) sts. Working both sides at same time, BO 2 sts at each neck edge once, dec 1 st at each neck edge EOR 2 times—14 (16, 19, 21) sts each shoulder. Cont in patt until piece measures 20 (21, 25, 26)". BO rem sts.

sleeves

CO 30 sts, work in St st for 6 rows. Cont in St st, inc 1 st each edge every 6 rows 11 times—52 sts. For better seams, make inc 2 sts from each edge. Cont until piece measures 17" or desired length. BO 4 sts at beg of next 10 rows. BO 12 rem sts.

finishing

Sew shoulder seams. Sew one sleeve with knit side out. Sew the other sleeve with purl side out. Sew side seams, leaving a 6" opening at the bottom edge on each side for slit. PU sts around slit edge and BO. Work 1 row of sc around neck edge.

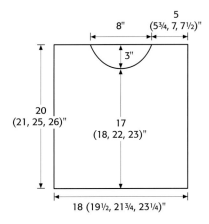

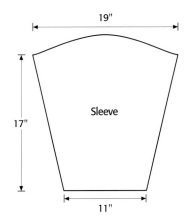

Holiday Haute Pullover

Glimmer and glitter in this glamorous sweater with faux fur.
Wearing this makes any day a holiday.

Skill Level: Beginner

Sizes: Extra Small (Small, Medium, Large, Extra Large)

Finished Bust Measurements: 38 (40, 42, 44, 48)"

materials

- **A** 8 (9, 10, 11, 12) skeins Trendsetter Yarns Dune (41% mohair, 30% acrylic, 12% viscose, 11% nylon, 6% metal; 90 yds/skein), color 92

- **B** 3 (3, 4, 4, 4) skeins Takhi Sable (70% merino wool, 30% French angora; 140 yds/skein), color 1612

- **C** 2 skeins Berroco Zap (100% polyester; 50 yds/skein), color 3553

- Size 17 needles (or size required to obtain gauge)

- Size 15 circular needle (24") for neck

GAUGE: 8 sts and 12 rows = 4" in St st on size 17 needles with
2 strands of A and 1 strand of B held tog (3 strands total)

---

melissa's point
Wear this to your next party or consider throwing a party yourself,
or just wear the pullover to work like I do.

skill builder

THE THIN eyelash-like strands of the Zap yarn will naturally go to the purl side. Strands can be "picked" to either side with a blunt needle to achieve the desired look.

back

With 2 strands of A and 1 strand of B held tog and size 17 needles, CO 38 (40, 42, 44, 48) sts. Work in St st until piece measures 12 (13, 14, 14, 15)". **Shape armholes:** BO 2 sts at beg of next 2 rows, dec 1 st at each end EOR 2 (2, 3, 3, 4) times—30 (32, 32, 34, 36) sts. Cont in St st until piece measures 20 (21, 22, 22, 23½)". BO all sts.

front

Work as for back until piece measures 17 (18, 19, 19, 20½)". **Shape neck:** Work across 10 (11, 11, 12, 13) sts, join a second ball of yarn and BO ctr 10 sts, work across rem 10 (11, 11, 12, 13) sts. Working both sides at same time, dec 1 st at neck edge EOR 2 (2, 2, 3, 3) times—8 (9, 9, 9, 10) sts for each shoulder. Cont until piece measures 20 (21, 22, 22, 23½)". BO rem sts.

sleeves

With 2 strands of C held tog and size 15 needles, CO 20 (20, 20, 22, 22) sts. Work 4 rows in garter st. Change to 2 strands of A and one strand of B held together and size 17 needle, work in St st, inc 1 st at each edge every 6 rows 4 (4, 5, 5, 6) times—28 (28, 30, 32, 34) sts. For better seams, work inc 2 sts from each edge. Cont until piece measures 16" or desired length. **Shape cap:** BO 2 sts at beg of next 2 rows, dec 1 st at each end EOR 9 (9, 10, 10, 10) times. BO rem 6 (6, 6, 8, 10) sts.

finishing

Sew shoulder seams. **Collar:** With size 15 circular needle and 2 strands of C held tog, PU 44 (44, 46, 46, 46) sts around neck edge (see page 15). Work 4 rows of garter st. Remember, when working in the round, that means *knit 1 row, purl 1 row; rep from *. Sew sleeve and side seams.

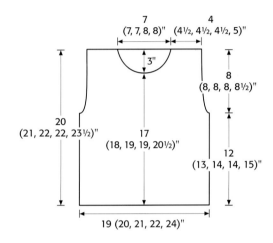

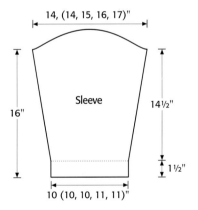

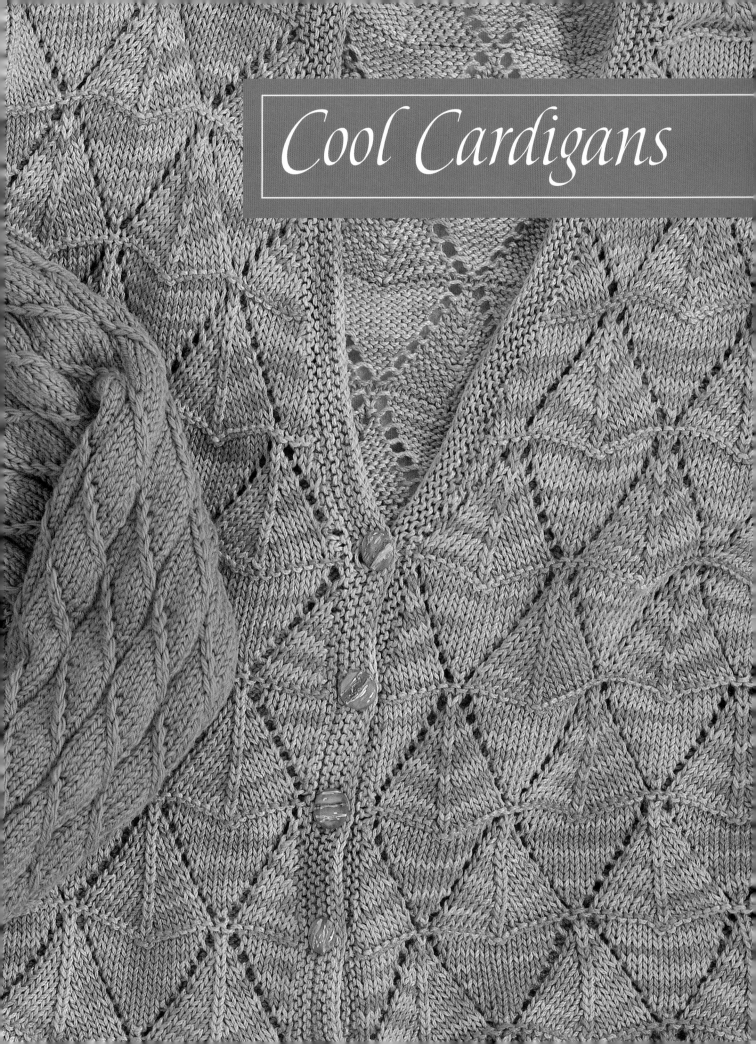

Cool Cardigans

Fake Cable Cardigan

Rich diagonal latticework creates a resilient dimension. A retro collar and buttons enhance the simple classic design.

Skill Level: Intermediate

Sizes: Small (Medium, Large, Extra Large)

Finished Bust Measurements: 39 (43, 47½, 53½)"

materials

- ◎ 18 (19, 20, 21) skeins Debbie Bliss Merino Aran (100% merino wool; 88 yds/skein), color 325201

- ◎ Size 5 needles (or size required to obtain gauge)

- ◎ Size 8 needles

- ◎ 5 buttons, 1" diameter

GAUGE: 24 sts and 24 rows = 4" in Fake Cable patt, slightly stretched, on size 8 needles

---

═ melissa's point ═
Fake is right. You have a beautiful cable look
without ever having to find that cable needle.

skill builder

*T*HE RIB and traveling stitch pull the fabric together. Work with worsted-weight yarn and do a swatch over the complete pattern stitch to obtain the correct gauge.

fake cable pattern (multiple of 9 +2)

C2L = Skip the first st on left-hand needle, knit in back of second st, twist right-hand needle and slip front st as if to knit, slipping both sts off left-hand needle.

Row 1: *P2, C2L, K5, rep from *, end P2.

Row 2 and all even rows: *K2, P7, rep from *, end K2.

Row 3: *P2, K1, C2L, K4, rep from *, end P2.

Row 5: *P2, K2, C2L, K3, rep from *, end P2.

Row 7: *P2, K3, C2L, K2, rep from *, end P2.

Row 9: *P2, K4, C2L, K1, rep from *, end P2.

Row 11: *P2, K5, C2L, rep from *, end P2.

Row 12: *K2, P7, rep from *, end K2.

Rep rows 1–12.

K1, P1 rib pattern

Row 1: K1, P1, rep from *, end K1.

Row 2: Knit the knit sts, purl the purl sts.

Rep row 2.

back

With size 5 needles, CO 119 (128, 137, 155) sts. Work in K1, P1 Rib patt for 1½". Change to size 8 needles, work Fake Cable patt until piece measures 12 (13½, 15½, 15½)". **Shape armholes**: BO 3 sts at beg of next 2 rows, BO 2 sts at beg of next 2 rows, dec 1 st at each edge EOR 4 (4, 8, 13) times—101 (110, 111, 119) sts. When piece measures 20½ (22, 24, 24)", BO rem sts in patt.

right front

With size 5 needles, CO 56 (65, 74, 83) sts. Work as for back until piece measures 12 (13½, 15½, 15½)". **Shape armhole**: BO 3 sts at side edge once, BO 2 sts at side edge once, dec 1 st at side edge EOR 4 (4, 8, 13) times—47 (56, 61, 65) sts. Cont in patt until piece measures 17½ (19, 21, 21)". **Shape neck**: BO 5 sts at neck edge once, BO 4 sts at neck edge once, BO 3 sts at neck edge once, BO 2 sts at neck edge once, dec 1 st at neck edge EOR 4 (6, 6, 6) times—29 (36, 41, 45) sts. Cont in patt until piece measures 20½ (22, 24, 24)". BO rem sts in patt.

left front

Work as for right front, reversing shaping.

sleeves

With size 5 needles, CO 52 (60, 60, 60) sts. Work in K1, P1 Rib patt for 1½", inc 13 (14, 14, 14) sts evenly across last row—65 (74, 74, 74) sts. Change to size 8 needles, work Fake Cable patt, inc 1 st at each edge every 4 rows 24 times—113 (122, 122, 122) sts. Cont in patt until piece measures 18" or desired length. **Shape cap**: BO 4 sts at beg of next 2 rows,

BO 3 sts at beg of next 2 rows, BO 2 sts at beg of next 2 rows, dec 1 st at each edge EOR 6 times. BO rem sts in patt.

finishing

Sew shoulder seams. **Right front band**: With size 5 needles, PU 68 sts along right front edge and work in K1, P1 Rib patt for 1¼", working 5 buttonholes into band as YO, K2 tog. BO all sts in patt. **Left front band**: Work as for right front band, omitting buttonholes. **Collar**: With size 5 needles, PU 40 (42, 45, 48) sts along front neck, 32 (34, 34, 34) sts along back neck, 40 (42, 45, 48) sts along front neck—112 (118, 124, 130) sts. Work in K1, P1 Rib patt for 3½". BO all sts in patt. Sew sleeve and side seams. Sew buttons on left front band to match buttonholes.

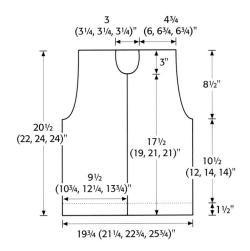

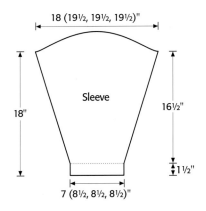

Diamond Lace Cardigan

This elegantly simple design makes for a flattering silhouette.

Skill Level: Intermediate

Sizes: Small (Medium, Large, Extra Large)

Finished Bust Measurements: 42 (48, 50, 56)"

materials

◎ 3 (3, 4, 4) skeins Schafer Yarns Laurel (100% mercerized pima cotton; 400 yds/skein), hand painted

◎ Size 10 needles (or size required to obtain gauge)

◎ Size 9 circular needle (36") for neck

◎ 6 buttons, ¾" diameter

GAUGE: 16 sts and 20 rows = 4" in Diamond Lace patt on size 10 needles

---

melissa's point

This might look like a challenge, but after the first diamond,
it becomes automatic and you won't even need to look at the pattern.
Try making it short; it really looks cool cropped.

diamond lace pattern (16-stitch repeat)

Row 1: Purl.

Row 2 and all even rows: Purl.

Row 3: K1, YO, K6, K3tog, K6, YO.

Row 5: K2, YO, K5, K3tog, K5, YO, K1.

Row 7: K3, YO, K4, K3tog, K4, YO, K2.

Row 9: K4, YO, K3, K3tog, K3, YO, K3.

Row 11: K5, YO, K2, K3tog, K2, YO, K4.

Row 13: K6, YO, K1, K3tog, K1, YO, K5.

Row 15: K7, YO, K3tog, YO, K6.

Row 17: Purl.

Row 19: K7, YO, K3tog, YO, K6.

Row 21: K6, YO, K1, K3tog, K1, YO, K5.

Row 23: K5, YO, K2, K3tog, K2, YO, K4.

Row 25: K4, YO, K3, K3tog, K3, YO, K3.

Row 27: K3, YO, K4, K3tog, K4, YO, K2.

Row 29: K2, YO, K5, K3tog, K5, YO, K1.

Row 31: K1, YO, K6, K3tog, K6, YO.

Row 32: Purl.

Rep rows 1–32.

 skill builder

Whard HEN KNITTING LACE, keep track of increases and decreases. Every increase needs to have a corresponding decrease. When increasing for the sleeves and there are not enough stitches to complete half the pattern-stitch repeat, work the remaining stitches in Stockinette stitch.

back

With size 10 needles, CO 80 (88, 96, 104) sts. Work 4 rows in garter st. **Foundation row:** Beg Diamond Lace patt and work a total of 5 (5½, 6, 6½) repeats. For Medium and Extra Large, work last 2 sts of the half rep as K2tog. When piece measures 5", CO 2 sts at each edge, work these sts in St st—84 (92, 100, 108) sts. Cont in patt until piece measures 24 (26, 28, 28)". BO all sts in patt.

right front

With size 10 needles, CO 40 (48, 48, 56) sts. Work 4 rows in garter st. **Foundation row:** Beg Diamond Lace patt and work a total of 2½ (3, 3, 3½) repeats. For Small and Extra Large, work last 2 sts of the half rep as K2tog. When piece measures 5", CO 2 sts at side edge only, work these sts in St st—42 (50, 50, 58) sts. Cont in patt until piece measures 16 (18, 20, 20)". **Shape neck:** Work dec row at neck edge, (K1, sl1, K1, psso, work in patt across row) EOR 18 times. Cont in patt until piece measures 24 (26, 28, 28)". BO 24 (32, 32, 40) sts in patt for shoulder.

left front

Work as for right front, reversing shaping. **Dec row:** Work to last 3 sts at neck edge, K2tog, K1.

sleeves

With size 10 needles, CO 40 (40, 48, 48) sts. Work 4 rows in garter st. Work foundation row as for front for 4". Cont in patt, inc 1 st at each edge every 4 rows 16 (16, 18, 19) times—72 (72, 84, 86) sts. For better seams, work inc 2 sts from each edge. Cont in patt until piece measures 16½" or desired length. BO all sts in patt.

finishing

Sew shoulder seams. **Front and neck band:** With size 9 circular needle and RS facing, PU 100 (108, 116, 116) sts along right front, 30 sts around neck, 100 (108, 116, 116) sts along left front—230 (246, 262, 262) sts. Work in garter st for 1", working 6 buttonholes in right front band (see page 17). BO all sts. Sew sleeve. Sew side seams, leaving 5" opening at bottom edge. With size 9 needle, PU a total of 40 sts along slit edges and work 2 rows garter st. BO all sts. Sew buttons on left front band to match buttonholes.

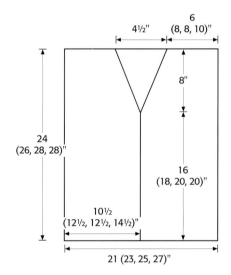

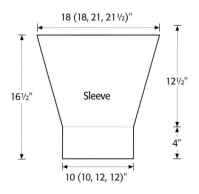

Zoom Wrap Cardigan

Add a touch of romance to your attire with this V-neck surplice.

Skill Level: Beginner

Sizes: Small (Medium, Large, Extra Large)

Finished Bust Measurements: 38½ (41, 43½, 46)"

materials

- ◉ **MC** 11 (12, 13 14) skeins Classic Elite Yarns Zoom (50% alpaca, 50% wool; 52 yds/skein), color 1010

- ◉ **CC** 2 skeins Ironstone Yarns Bouquet of Colors Mohair Loop (90% mohair, 5% wool, 5% nylon; 75 yds/skein), color 100

- ◉ Size 10 needles (or size required to obtain gauge)

- ◉ Size 7 needles

- ◉ Size J crochet hook

GAUGE: 13 sts and 18 rows = 4" in St st with Zoom on size 10 needles.

---

melissa's point
A beautiful leather belt would look
fabulous on this cardigan.

 *skill builder*

To INCREASE the size and fullness of the collar, continue to increase 1 stitch before each marker every 4 rows until the desired length and fullness is reached.

back

With size 7 needles and CC, CO 62 (66, 70, 74) sts. Work in garter st for 6 rows. Change to size 10 needles and MC, work in St st until piece measures 11½ (13, 14½, 16)". **Shape armholes:** BO 3 (3, 4, 4) sts at beg of next 2 rows, BO 2 sts at beg of next 2 rows, dec 1 st at each edge 2 (2, 3, 4) times—48 (52, 52, 54) sts. Cont until piece measures 20½ (22, 24, 26½)". BO all sts.

right front

With size 7 needles and CC, CO 40 (42, 44, 46) sts. Work in garter st for 6 rows. Change to size 10 needles and MC, work in St st for 6 rows. **Front edge shaping:** Dec 1 st every 6 rows 6 (7, 8, 9) times—34 (35, 36, 37) sts. Cont until piece measures 11 (12½, 14, 15½)". **Shape neck:** Dec 1 st every 4 rows 10 (10, 8, 8) times. At the same time when piece measures 11½ (13, 14½, 16)", **shape armhole:** BO 3 (3, 4, 4) sts at beg of next side edge, BO 2 sts at beg of next side edge, BO 1 st at beg of next 2 (2, 4, 4) side edges—17 (18, 18, 19) sts. Cont until piece measures 20½ (22, 24, 26½)". BO rem sts.

left front

Work as for right front, reversing shaping.

sleeves

With size 7 needles and CC, CO 26 (28, 28, 30) sts. Work in garter st for 6 rows. Change to size 10 needles and MC, work in St st, inc 1 st each end every 4 rows 13 (14, 15, 15) times—52 (56, 58, 60) sts. For better seams, work inc 2 sts from each edge. When piece measures 17" or desired length, **shape cap:** BO 3 sts at beg of next 12 rows. BO rem sts.

finishing

Sew shoulder, side, and sleeve seams.

Collar: With size 7 needles and CC, PU 150 (158, 164, 168) sts along fronts and neck edge. Work in garter st for 4 rows. BO 35 sts along front edge before V-neck shaping, beg of next 2 rows. Change to size 10 needles, cont in garter st along V neck and back edge to shape lapels, dec 1 st at beg of next 10 rows. **Shape collar:** BO 8 sts at beg of next 2 rows. Evenly space 3 markers across next row. Inc 1 st before marker every 4 rows. When collar measures 6", BO all sts loosely.
Belt: With MC, crochet a chain 55" long and work rows of single crochet until belt is ½" wide.

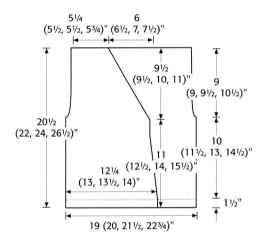

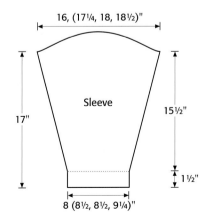

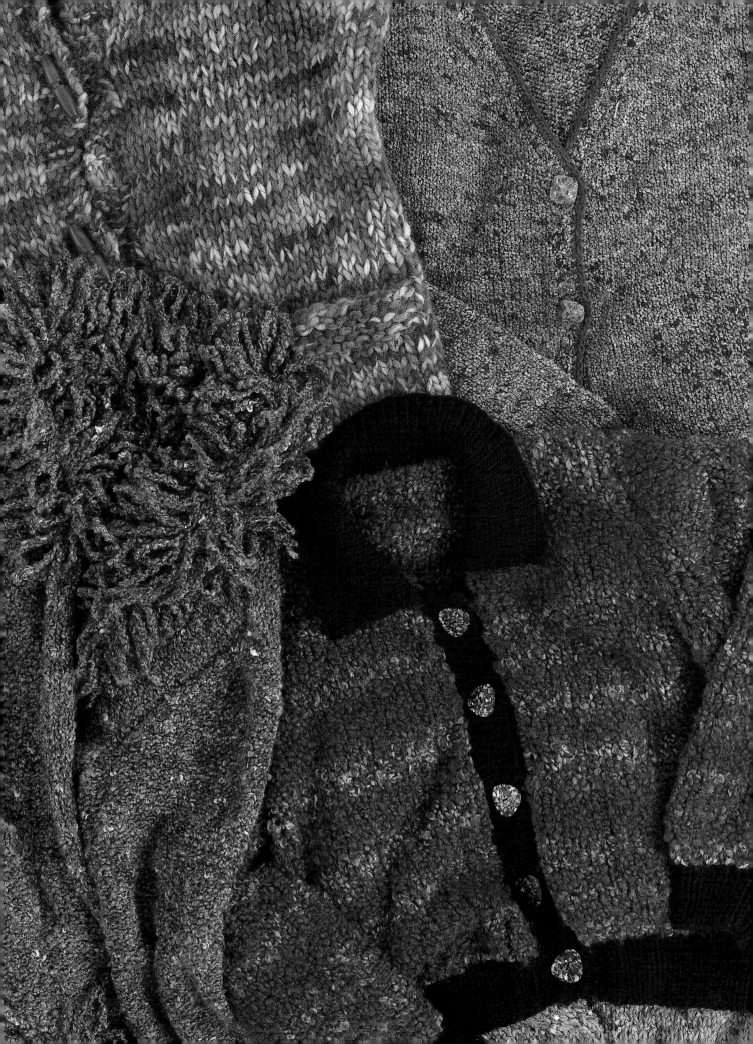

Jazzy Jackets

Faux Astrakhan Jacket

Contrasting trim accents this cropped jacket with a European flair.

Skill Level: Beginner

Sizes: Small (Medium, Large, Extra Large)

Finished Bust Measurements: 38 (41, 44, 47)"

materials

- **MC** 10 (11, 12, 13) skeins S. Charles Verona (36% cotton, 24% viscose, 20% wool, 10% acrylic, 10% polyamide; 60 yds/skein), color 5

- **CC** 1 skein Berroco Mohair Classic (78% mohair, 13% wool, 9% nylon; 93 yds/skein), color 1106

- Size 9 needles (or size required to obtain gauge)

- 5 buttons, ⅝" diameter

GAUGE: 10.4 sts and 16 rows = 4" in St st with Verona

---

melissa's point

This is a great dress-up or dress-down jacket.
It's so quick and easy to make.

 *skill builder*

COMBINING TWO strands of worsted yarns can be substituted for a single yarn in this pattern. Be sure to swatch to obtain the correct gauge.

K1, P1 rib pattern

Row 1: K1, P1, rep from *, end K1.
Row 2: Knit the knit sts, purl the purl sts.
Rep row 2.

back

With MC, CO 44 (48, 52, 56) sts. Work in St st, inc 1 st at each edge every 6 (6, 8, 8) rows 3 times—50 (54, 58, 62) sts. Cont until piece measures 11 (13, 15, 15)". **Shape armholes:** BO 3 sts at beg of next 2 rows, dec 1 st at each edge EOR 3 times—38 (42, 46, 50) sts. Cont until piece measures 20 (22, 24, 24)". BO all sts.

right front

With MC, CO 22 (24, 26, 28) sts. Work in St st, inc 1 st at side edge only every 6 (6, 8, 8) rows 3 times—25 (27, 29, 31) sts. Cont until piece measures 11 (13, 15, 15)". **Shape armhole:** BO 3 sts at side edge once, dec 1 st at side edge EOR 3 times—19 (21, 23, 25) sts. Cont until piece measures 17 (19, 21, 21)". **Shape neck:** BO 5 sts at neck edge once, BO 2 sts at neck edge once, dec 1 st at neck edge EOR 3 (3, 4, 4) times—9 (11, 12, 14) sts. Cont until piece measures 20 (22, 24, 24)". BO all sts.

left front

Work as for right front, reversing shaping.

sleeves

With CC, CO 28 (28, 30, 30) sts. Work in St st, dec 1 st at each edge every 4 rows 3 times until piece measures 3½"—22 (22, 24, 24) sts. Change to MC, work in K1, P1 Rib patt for 2". Beg St st, inc 4 sts evenly across row—26 (26, 28, 28) sts. Cont in St st, inc 1 st at each edge every 4 rows 8 (9, 10, 10) times—42 (44, 48, 48) sts. For better seams, work inc 2 sts from each edge. Cont until piece measures 19½ (19½, 20½, 21)". **Shape cap:** BO 3 sts at beg of next 2 rows, dec 1 st at each edge EOR 13 (14, 16, 16) times. BO rem sts.

finishing

Sew shoulder seams. **Collar:** With CC, PU 42 (42, 44, 44) sts around neck edge, work in St st, inc 1 st at each end every 4 rows 3 times—48 (48, 50, 50) sts. Cont until piece measures 4½". BO all sts. **Right front band:** With MC, PU 40 (44, 48, 52) sts along right front edge, work garter st for 1¼", working 5 buttonholes in band (see page 17). BO all sts. **Left front band:** Work as for right front band, omitting buttonholes. Sew sleeve and fold cuff back. Sew side seams. Sew buttons on left front band to match buttonholes.

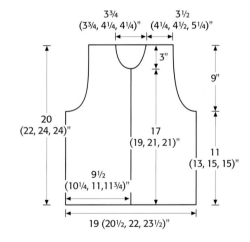

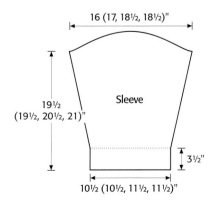

Italian Jacket

Artful and refined trim define this beautifully tailored jacket.

Skill Level: Beginner

Sizes: Small (Medium, Large, Extra Large)

Finished Bust Measurements: 37 (40, 44, 48)"

materials

- **MC** 12 (13, 14, 15) skeins Filatura di Crosa Cipresso (55% wool, 27% viscose, 10% acrylic, 8% polyamid; 71.5 yds/skein), color 11

- **CC** 1 skein Crystal Palace Cotton Chenille (100% cotton; 109 yds/skein), color 2810

- Size 10 needles (or size required to obtain gauge)

- Size I crochet hook

- 4 buttons, 1" diameter

- 4 buttons, ¾" diameter

- Stitch holder

GAUGE: 14.8 sts and 20 rows = 4" in St st with Cipresso

---

melissa's point
This style is classic, with its distinctive nubby texture,
signature-trim edges, and close-fitting silhouette.

 skill builder

_F_OLLOW THE directions for the flaps to work the gauge swatches.

back

With MC, CO 68 (74, 82, 90) sts. Work in St st for 6 rows. Cont in St st, dec 1 st at each edge every 6 rows 4 times—60 (66, 74, 82) sts. Work 6 rows even. Cont in St st, inc 1 st at each edge every 6 rows 4 times—68 (74, 82, 90) sts. Cont until piece measures 12 (13, 14, 14)". **Shape armholes:** BO 5 sts at beg of next 2 rows, dec 1 st at each edge EOR 6 (7, 8, 9) times—46 (50, 56, 62) sts. Cont until piece measures 20 (21, 22, 22)". BO sts loosely.

right front

With MC, CO 34 (38, 42, 46) sts. Work in St st for 6 rows. Cont in St st, dec 1 st at side edge only every 6 rows 4 times—30 (34, 38, 42) sts. Work 6 rows even. Cont in St st, inc 1 st at side edge only every 6 rows 4 times—34 (38, 42, 46) sts. Cont until piece measures 12 (13, 14, 14)". **Shape armhole:** BO 5 sts at side edge once, dec 1 st at side edge EOR 6 (7, 8, 9) times—23 (26, 29, 32) sts. Cont until piece measures 14 (15, 16, 16)". **Shape neck:** Dec 1 st at neck edge EOR 11 times—12 (15, 18, 21) sts. Cont until piece measures 20 (21, 22, 22)". BO sts loosely.

left front

Work as for right front, reversing shaping.

flaps

With MC, CO 15 sts. Work in St st, inc 1 st at each edge every 4 rows 2 times—19 sts. Work 4 rows even. BO all sts. With CC, work 1 row single crochet around sides and CO edge.

sleeves

With MC, CO 13 sts for RS of cuff. Work in St st for 4", ending on WS row; place sts on holder. **Left side of cuff:** CO 26 sts; work in St st for 4", ending on WS row. **Joining row (RS):** K10 sts from holder, hold rem 3 sts at back, and work first 3 sts of left side as follows: Knit 1 st from left side tog with 1 st from holder 3 times, knit to end. Cont in St st, inc 1 st at each edge every 8 rows 12 (12, 14, 15) times—60 (60, 64, 66) sts. For better seams, work inc 2 sts from each edge. Cont

until piece measures 16 (16½, 16½, 17)".
Shape cap: BO 4 sts at beg of next 2 rows, dec 1 st at each edge EOR 8 (8, 10, 11) times, BO 3 sts at beg of next 4 rows. BO rem sts. Make second sleeve, reversing cuff.

finishing

Sew shoulder, sleeve, and side seams. With CC, work 1 row single crochet around all edges. On right front edge, work 4 button-holes by making 1 chain at desired button-hole placement. Sew flaps on each front, positioning over hip bone. Sew larger buttons on left front band to match buttonholes. Sew a smaller button on each cuff and flap.

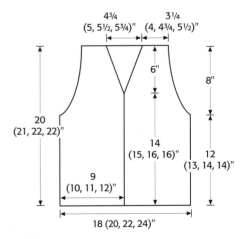

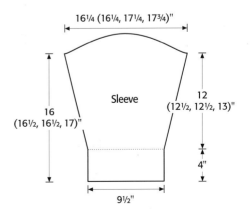

Little Zip Jacket

This smart little jacket zips for exceptional comfort with a chic look.

Skill Level: Beginner

Sizes: Extra Small (Small, Medium, Large, Extra Large)

Finished Bust Measurements: 36½ (39, 42, 46, 50½)"

materials

- **A**　7 (7, 8, 9, 10) skeins S. Charles Cancun (68% polyester, 8% cotton, 10% polyamid, 14% viscose; 93 yds/skein), color 50

- **B**　6 (7, 8, 8, 9) skeins Debbie Bliss Cashmerino Aran (55% merino wool, 33% microfiber, 12% cashmere; 99 yds/skein), color 300503

- Size 10½ needles (or size required to obtain gauge)

- Size J crochet hook

- Separating zipper

GAUGE: 11.4 sts and 16 rows = 4" in St st with 1 strand of A and B held tog

---

melissa's point
Since it's everyone's favorite, I make this jacket
every season using the latest yarn.

WHEN WORKING with two yarns, join yarns at the end of a row when needed. It is not necessary to join both balls at the same time.

back

With 1 strand of A and B held tog, CO 46 (50, 54, 60, 66) sts. Work in St st, inc 1 st at each edge every 8 rows 3 times—52 (56, 60, 66, 72) sts. Cont until piece measures 11 (13, 14, 14, 15)". **Shape armholes:** BO 4 sts at beg of next 2 rows, dec 1 st at each edge EOR 2 times—40 (44, 48, 54, 60) sts. Cont until piece measures 19 (21½, 22½, 23, 24)". BO all sts.

right front

With 1 strand of A and B held tog, CO 23 (25, 27, 30, 33) sts. Work in St st, inc 1 st at side edge only every 8 rows 3 times—26 (28, 30, 33, 36) sts. Cont until piece measures 11 (13, 14, 14, 15)". **Shape armhole:** BO 4 sts at side edge once, dec 1 st at side edge EOR 2 times—20 (22, 24, 27, 30) sts. Cont until piece measures 16 (18½, 19½, 20, 21)". **Shape neck:** BO 5 sts at neck edge once, BO 3 sts at neck edge once, BO 2 sts at neck edge once, dec 1 st at neck edge once—9 (11, 13, 16, 19) sts. Cont until piece measures 19 (21½, 22½, 23, 24)". BO rem sts.

left front

Work as for right front, reversing shaping.

sleeves

With 1 strand of A and B held tog, CO 30 (30, 32, 32, 34) sts. Work in St st, inc 1 st at each edge every 6 rows 7 (7, 7, 8, 8) times—44 (44, 46, 48, 50) sts. For better seams, work inc 2 sts from each edge. Cont until piece measures 15½ (16, 16½, 16½, 17)" or desired length. **Shape cap:** BO 3 sts at beg of next 2 rows, dec 1 st at each edge EOR 7 times, BO 3 sts at beg of next 6 rows. BO rem sts.

finishing

Sew shoulder, sleeve, and side seams. With 2 strands of B, work 1 row of single crochet around all edges; then work 1 row of shrimp stitch (see page 15). Sew in zipper (see page 18).

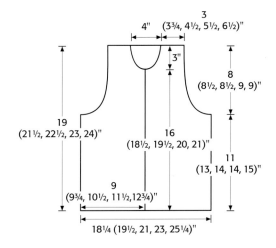

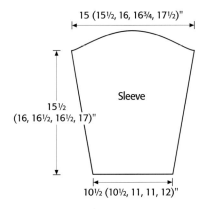

Flair Jacket

Come out smiling in this uniquely trimmed jacket. Make it short or long. It's sure to add a little finesse to your wardrobe.

Skill Level: Beginner

Sizes: Extra Small (Small, Medium, Large, Extra Large)

Finished Bust Measurements: 36 (40, 44, 48, 52)"

materials

SHORT

- **A**   8 (8, 9, 9, 10) skeins Ironstone Yarns Flecia (71% cotton, 29% rayon; 142 yds/skein), color 307

- **B**   11 (11, 12, 12, 13) skeins Crystal Palace Yarns Wakiki (70% rayon, 30% cotton; 105 yds/skein), color 2889

- 7 buttons, ½" diameter

LONG

14 (15, 16, 17, 18) skeins Ironstone Rustic Tweed (rayon, polyester, acrylic; 90 yds/ skein), color 2

BOTH VERSIONS

Size 10½ needles (or size required to obtain gauge)

Size K crochet hook

4" prop for loops (something to wrap loops around such as a piece of cardboard or a makeup compact)

GAUGE: 12 sts and 16 rows = 4" in St st (For short version, work 1 strand of A and B held tog. For long version, work 1 strand of Rustic Tweed.)

CROCHET LOOP PATTERN

Row 1 (RS): Single crochet across row.

Row 2 (WS): Make loop as follows: *insert hook and YO, pulling yarn to front of work; adjust the loop to fit the 4" prop; YO with hook and yarn in front of loop and complete the st; rep from * across row.

Rep rows 1 and 2.

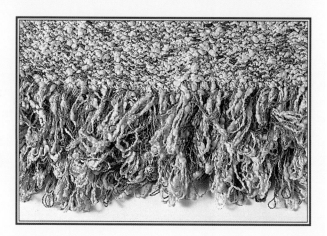

— Short Version —

back

With 1 strand of A and B held tog, CO 54 (60, 66, 72, 78) sts. Work in St st for 6 rows. Cont in St st, dec 1 st at each edge every 6 rows 3 times—50 (56, 60, 66, 72) sts. Work 6 rows even. Cont in St st, inc 1 st at each edge every 6 rows 3 times—54 (60, 66, 72, 78) sts. Cont until piece measures 12 (12, 13, 13, 13)". **Shape armholes:** BO 4 sts at beg of next 2 rows, BO 2 sts at beg of next 2 rows, dec 1 st at each edge EOR 2 times—38 (44, 50, 56, 62) sts. Cont until piece measures 20 (20, 21, 21, 21)". BO all sts.

right front

With 1 strand of A and B held tog, CO 27 (30, 33, 36, 39) sts. Work in St st for 6 rows. Cont in St st, dec 1 st at side edge every 6 rows 3 times—24 (27, 30, 33, 36) sts. Work 6 rows even. Cont in St st, inc 1 st at side edge every 6 rows 3 times—27 (30, 33, 36, 39) sts. Cont until piece measures 12 (12, 13, 13, 13)". **Shape armhole:** BO 4 sts at side edge once, BO 2 sts at side edge once, dec 1 st at side edge EOR 2 times—19 (22, 25, 28, 31) sts. Cont until piece measures 13 (13, 14, 14, 14)". **Shape neck:** Dec 1 st at neck edge EOR 10 (11, 12, 14, 16) times—9 (11, 13, 14, 15) sts. Cont until piece measures 20 (20, 21, 21, 21)". BO rem sts.

left front

Work as for right front, reversing shaping.

— Long Version —

back

With 1 strand of Rustic Tweed, CO 54 (60, 66, 72, 78) sts. Work in St st for 8 rows. Cont in St st, dec 1 st at each edge every 8 rows 3 times—48 (54, 60, 66, 72) sts. Work 8 rows even. Cont in St st, inc 1 st at each edge every 8 rows 3 times—54 (60, 66, 72, 78) sts. Cont until piece measures 17". **Shape armhole:** BO 4 sts at beg of next 2 rows, BO 2 sts at beg of next 2 rows, dec 1 st at each edge EOR 2 times—38 (44, 50, 56, 62) sts. Cont until piece measures 25". BO all sts.

right front

With 1 strand of Rustic Tweed, CO 27 (30, 33, 36, 39) sts. Work in St st for 8 rows. Cont in St st, dec 1 st at side edge every 8 rows 3 times—24 (27, 30, 33, 36) sts. Work 8 rows even. Cont in St st, inc 1 st at side edge every 8 rows 3 times—27 (30, 33, 36, 39) sts. Cont until piece measures 17". **Shape armhole:** BO 4 sts at side edge once, BO 2 sts at side edge once, dec 1 st EOR 2 times—19 (22, 25, 28, 31) sts. Cont until piece measures 18". **Shape neck:** Dec 1 st at neck edge EOR 10 (11, 12, 14, 16) times—9 (11, 13, 14, 15) sts. Cont until piece measures 25". BO rem sts.

left front

Work as for right front, reversing shaping.

sleeves for short and long versions

With 1 strand of A and B held tog for the short version, and 1 strand of Rustic Tweed for the long, CO 27 (27, 31, 31, 31) sts. Work in St st, inc 1 st at each edge every 6 rows 8 (8, 9, 10, 10) times—43 (43, 49, 51, 51) sts. For better seams, work inc 2 sts from each edge. Cont until piece measures 16½" or desired length. **Shape cap:** BO 4 sts at beg of next 2 rows, dec 1 st at each edge EOR 10 (10, 11, 11, 11) times. BO 2 sts at beg of next 2 rows. BO rem sts.

finishing for short and long versions

Sew shoulder, sleeve, and side seams. Work Crochet Loop patt around bottom and cuff bands: Crochet total of 11 rows of Crochet Loop patt. **Collar:** Crochet total of 13 rows of

Crochet Loop patt, dec 2 sts at each edge on each row. For short version, sew buttons to left front; buttonholes are not necessary as the small buttons can be worked through the knit fabric. For belt on long version, crochet a chain 55" long with 1 strand of Rustic Tweed and work rows of single crochet until the belt is 1¼" wide.

pocket on long version (make 2)

With size 10 needle, CO 14 sts and work in St st until piece measures 5". Change to K1, P1 rib, work 4 rows. BO all sts in patt. Sew in place on bottom fronts.

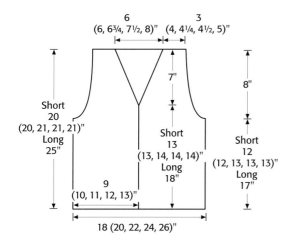

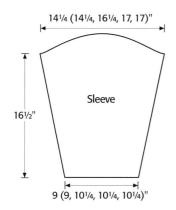

Worn with Twice As Nice Tank, page 42.

- ◉ **MC**–12 (13, 14, 15, 15) skeins Trendsetter Yarns Vintage (60% polyamid, 40% Tactel nylon; 95 yds/skein), color 4384

- ◉ **CC**–2 Skeins Trendsetter Yarns Marabella (50% polyamid, 50% Tactel nylon; 93 yds/skein), color 4207

Worked as short version using Vintage yarn single.

Finishing: With 2 strands CC held tog, work 1 row of single crochet around all edges; then work 1 row of shrimp stitch (see page 15).

Houndstooth Jacket

The combination of dramatic checks and modern styling in this fashion-able, yet functional jacket provides a sophisticated silhouette.

Skill Level: Intermediate

Sizes: Small (Medium, Large, Extra Large)

Finished Bust Measurements: 41 (45, 48, 51)"

materials

◎ **A**   9 (9, 10, 11) skeins Filatura di Crosa Luna (100% virgin wool; 88 yds/skein), color 224

◎ **B**   8 (8, 9, 10) skeins Filatura di Crosa Cipresso (55% wool, 27% viscose, 10% acrylic, 8% polyamid; 71.5 yds/skein), color 24

◎ Size 9 needles (or size required to obtain gauge)

◎ Size H crochet hook

◎ Separating zipper

◎ 2 buttons, ¾" diameter

◎ Stitch holder

GAUGE: 16 sts and 20 rows = 4" in Houndstooth patt

══ melissa's point ══
Slip-stitching is pure joy. Each row is worked with only one yarn.
Two yarns in the same row is merely an illusion.

skill builder

When slipping stitches, slip the stitch as if to purl, with the yarn in back, unless stated differently in the pattern.

houndstooth pattern

Cast on with A.

Row 1: With B, *K2, sl 1 wyib; rep from * to end.

Row 2: With B, purl.

Row 3: With A, K1, *sl 1 wyib, K2; rep from * to end.

Row 4: With A, purl.

Rep rows 1–4.

back

With A, CO 82 (90, 96, 102) sts. Work Houndstooth patt for 8 rows. Cont in patt, dec 1 st at each edge every 8 rows 3 times—76 (84, 90, 96) sts. Work 8 rows even. Cont in patt, inc 1 st every 8 rows 3 times—82 (90, 96, 102) sts. For better seams, work inc 2 sts from each edge. Cont until piece measures 14 (15½, 17, 18)". **Shape armholes:** BO 4 sts at beg of next 2 rows, BO 2 sts at beg of next 2 rows. Work dec row (K2, K2tog, knit to last 4 sts, sl 1, K1, psso, K2) EOR 3 times, then every 4 rows 1 (3, 5, 7) times—62 (66, 68, 70) sts. Cont until piece measures 21½ (23½, 25½, 27)". BO rem sts.

right front

With A, cast on 41 (45, 48, 51) sts. Work Houndstooth patt for 8 rows. Cont in patt, dec 1 st at side edge every 8 rows 3 times—38 (42, 45, 48) sts. Work 8 rows even. Cont in patt, inc 1 st at side edge every 8 rows 3 times—41 (45, 48, 51) sts. Cont until piece measures 14 (15½, 17, 18)". **Shape armhole:** BO 4 sts at side edge once, BO 2 sts at side edge once. Work dec row (RS) (K2, K2tog at side edge, work across row) EOR 3 times, then every 4 rows 1 (3, 5, 7) times—31 (33, 34, 35) sts. Cont until piece measures 18½ (20½, 22½, 24)". **Shape neck:** BO 6 (6, 7, 8) sts at neck edge once, BO 4 sts at neck edge once, dec 1 st at neck edge EOR 4 times—17 (19, 19, 19) sts. Cont until piece measures 21½ (23½, 25½, 27)". BO rem sts.

left front

Work as for right front, reversing shaping. Dec row (RS): Knit to last 4 sts, sl 1, K1, psso, K2.

sleeves

With A, CO 19 (19, 22, 22) sts for RS of cuff. Work in Houndstooth patt for 16 rows, ending on WS row; place sts on holder. **Left side of cuff:** CO 23 (23, 26, 26) sts. Work in patt, inc 1 st at end of every RS row 3 times until 16 rows are completed, ending on WS row—26 (26, 29, 29) sts. **Joining row (RS):** K15 (15, 18, 18) sts from holder, hold rem 4 sts at back, and work first 4 sts of left side as follows: K1 from left side tog with 1 st from holder 4 times, knit to end—41 (41, 47, 47) sts. Cont in patt, inc 1 st at each edge every 4 rows 8 (8, 10, 10) times, inc 1 st at each edge every 6 rows 5 times—67 (67, 77, 77) sts. Cont in patt until piece measures 17" or desired length. **Shape cap:** BO 2 sts at beg of next 2 rows, dec 1 st at each edge every 4 rows 3 times, dec 1 st at each edge EOR 10 times, BO 3 sts at beg of next 4 rows. BO rem sts. Make second sleeve, reversing cuff.

finishing

Sew shoulder, sleeve, and side seams. With B, work 1 row of single crochet around all edges; then work 1 row of shrimp stitch (see page 15). Sew in zipper (see page 18). Sew a button to each cuff through both thicknesses.

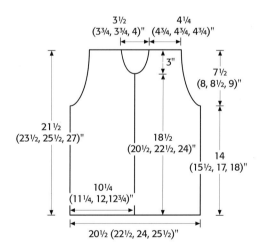

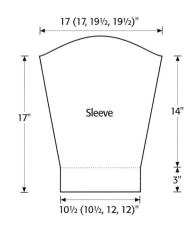

Baseball Jacket

This jacket is as American as the game it's named after.
But there's no need to play; just look great in this soft
and fluffy jacket with contrasting trim.

Skill Level: Intermediate

Sizes: Extra Small (Small, Medium, Large, Extra Large)

Finished Bust Measurements: 39 (42½, 46, 49½, 53)"

materials

- **A**   9 (10, 11, 12, 13) skeins Trendsetter Yarns Biscotto (60% acrylic, 40% wool; 40 yds/skein), color 15

- **B**   1 skein Brown Sheep Lambs Pride (85% wool, 15% mohair; 190 yds/skein), color M-05

- Size 10½ needles (or size required to obtain gauge)

- Size 7 needles

- 5 buttons, 1¼" diameter

GAUGE: 9 sts and 12 rows = 4" in St st with Biscotto on size 10½ needles

melissa's point

You can change the collar and have a different look.
Pick up the same number of stitches and work rib for only 1¼".
The result is a classic look.

K1, P1 rib pattern

Row 1: K1, P1, rep from *, end K1.

Row 2: Knit the knit sts, purl the purl sts.

Rep row 2.

back

With size 7 needles and A, CO 74 (78, 82, 86, 90) sts. Work in K1, P1 Rib patt for 2½", dec 30 sts evenly across next row—44 (48, 52, 56, 60) sts. Change to size 10½ needles and B, work in St st until piece measures 13". **Shape armholes:** BO 3 sts at beg of next 2 rows, dec 1 st at each edge EOR 1 (3, 4, 5, 6) times—36 (36, 38, 40, 42) sts. Cont until piece measures 22". BO all sts.

right front

With size 7 needles and A, CO 37 (39, 41, 43, 45) sts. Work K1, P1 Rib patt for 2½", dec 15 sts evenly across next row—22 (24, 26, 28, 30) sts. Change to size 10½ needles and B, work in St st until piece measures 13". **Shape armhole**: BO 3 sts at side edge once, dec 1 st at side edge 1 (3, 4, 5, 6) times—18 (18, 19, 20, 21) sts. Cont until piece measures 19". **Shape neck**: BO 4 (4, 5, 5, 5) sts at neck edge once, BO 2 sts at neck edge once, dec 1 st at neck edge EOR 2 times—10 (10, 10, 11, 12) sts. Cont until piece measures 22". BO rem sts.

left front

Work as for right front, reversing shaping.

sleeves

With size 7 needles and A, CO 38 (38, 40, 42, 42) sts. Work K1, P1 Rib patt for 2½", dec 14 sts evenly across next row—24 (24, 26, 28, 28) sts. Change to size 10½ needles and B, work in St st, inc 1 st at each edge every 4 rows 8 (8, 8, 9, 9) times—40 (40, 42, 46, 46) sts. Cont until piece measures 16 (16, 17, 17, 17)" or desired length. **Shape cap**: BO 3 sts at beg of next 2 rows, dec 1 st at each edge EOR 9 (9, 10, 12, 12) times, BO 2 sts at beg of next 4 rows. BO rem sts.

finishing

Sew shoulder seams. **Collar**: With size 7 needles and 2 strands of A held tog, PU 46 sts evenly around neck edge (see page 15). Work 1 st in each strand of yarn to get to 92 sts as follows: Knit into the first strand and purl into the second strand. Work in K1, P1 Rib patt for 4". BO in patt. Sew sleeve and side seams. **Right front band**: With size 7 needles and 2 strands of A held tog, PU 40 sts along right front and work 1 st in each strand as for neck edge—80 sts. Work in K1, P1 Rib patt for 1½", working 5 buttonholes in band (see page 17). **Left front band**: Work as for right front band, omitting buttonholes. Sew buttons on left front band to match buttonholes.

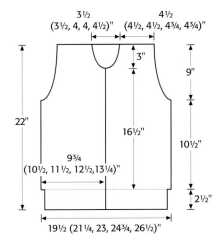

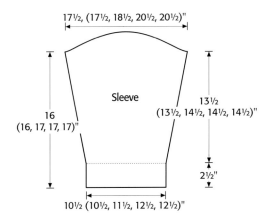

Cozy Jacket with Hood

Give everyone your warmest regards as you cuddle in comfort in this hooded jacket.

Skill Level: Intermediate

Sizes: Small (Medium, Large, Extra Large)

Finished Bust Measurements: 40 (42, 46, 50)"

materials

- 5 (6, 6, 7) skeins Plymouth Yarn Italian Fingerpaint (98% fine wool, 2% nylon; 132 yds/skein), color 1217
- Size 17 needles (or size required to obtain gauge)
- Size 15 needles
- Stitch holder
- 5 barrel buttons

GAUGE: 8 sts and 12 rows = 4" on size 17 needles

melissa's point

This jacket is perfect for stepping out for a breath of fresh air
or a walk in the woods with that special someone.
In my case it's with Trooper, my golden retriever.

THREE-NEEDLE BIND OFF

PLACE HALF the stitches on one needle and half on a second needle. With right sides together, hold both needles with the knitting in your left hand. Place a third needle in your right hand. Insert the right-hand needle into the first stitch on the front needle, and then into the first stitch on the back needle, knit the two stitches together at the same time. Repeat with the next two stitches on left-hand needles; then bind off in the usual manner, loosely. Continue knitting two stitches together from front and back needles and binding off across the row. When one stitch remains on right-hand needle, cut tail and pass through last loop.

Knit together one stitch from front needle and one stitch from back needle.

Bind off.

back

With size 15 needles, CO 40 (42, 46, 50) sts, work in garter st for 6 rows. Change to size 17 needles and work in St st until piece measures 21". **Shape armholes:** BO 2 sts at beg of next 2 rows. Dec 1 st at each edge EOR 3 times as follows: K1, sl 1, K1, psso, knit to last 3 sts, K2tog, K1—30 (32, 36, 40) sts. Work even until piece measures 29". BO all sts loosely.

pocket lining (make 2)

With size 15 needles, CO 10 sts and work in St st until piece measures 7". Place sts on holder.

left front

With size 15 needles, CO 23 (24, 26, 28) sts, work in garter st for 6 rows. Change to size 17 needles. Maintain ctr front edge (button band) in garter st for 4 sts, work across row in St st. Cont even until piece measures 8½". Prepare pocket placement:

Rows 1, 3, 5: Knit.

Rows 2, 4, 6: P4, K10, P5 (6, 8, 10), K4.

Place Pocket

Row 1: K9 (10, 12, 14), BO 10 sts, knit to end.

Row 2: P4, P10 sts of pocket lining from holder, P5 (6, 8, 10), K4.

Cont in St st maintaining ctr front 4 sts in garter st until piece measures 21". **Shape armhole:** BO 2 sts at beg of next side edge. Dec 1 st at side edge EOR 3 times as follows: K1, slip 1, K1, psso, work in patt to end—18 (19,

21, 23) sts. Work even until piece measures 26". **Shape neck:** BO 4 sts at neck edge once, BO 3 sts at neck edge once, dec 1 st at neck edge EOR 2 times—BO 9 (10, 12, 14) sts loosely.

Buttonholes are not necessary; the buttons can easily be pushed through the openings between stitches.

right front

Work as for left front, reversing shaping. **Armhole dec row:** Work in patt to last 3 sts, K2tog, K1.

sleeves

With size 15 needles, CO 17 (17, 19, 19) sts, work in garter st for 6 rows. Change to size 17 needles and beg St st. Work 6 rows, inc 1 st at each edge every 6 rows 5 times. For better seams, work inc 2 sts from edge. When piece measures 16½" or desired length, **shape cap:** BO 2 sts at beg of next 2 rows, work even 2 rows, dec 1 st at each edge EOR 8 times, BO 2 sts at beg of next 2 rows. BO rem sts.

finishing

Sew shoulder seams. **Hood:** PU 12 sts along right neck edge, 14 sts along back neck edge, 12 sts along left front neck edge—38 sts. To establish patt, work 4 sts in garter st, 30 sts in St st, 4 sts in garter st. Work 4 rows. Work 17 sts in patt, M1, K2, M1, work to end—40 sts. Work 7 rows even. Work 18 sts, M1, K2, M1, work to end—42sts. Work even until hood measures 11", ending on WS row. On RS row work 18 sts, SSK, K2, K2tog, work to end. Work 1 row even. Work 16 sts, SSK, K2, K2tog, work to end. Work 1 row even. Divide sts in half and use 3-needle BO method (see page 140). Sew sleeve and side seams.

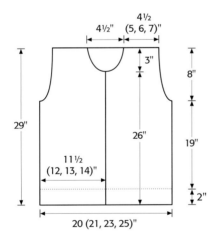

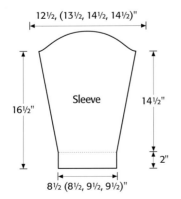

Abbreviations

beg	begin
BO	bind off
CC	contrasting color
cn	cable needle
CO	cast on
cont	continue
ctr	center
dec	decrease (decrease either by inserting needle into 2 stitches at once and knit or purl together, or slip 1 as if to knit, knit 1, pass slip stitch over)
EOR	every other row
est	established
garter st	knit every row
inc	increase (increase by working into front and back of same stitch)
K	knit
K2tog	knit 2 together
MC	main color
M1	make 1 stitch

P	purl
patt	pattern
psso	pass slip stitch over
PU	pick up and knit
rem	remaining
rep	repeat
rev St st	reverse stockinette stitch (purl 1 row, knit 1 row; repeat)
RS	right side
sl st	slip stitch
SSK	slip, slip, knit the 2 slip stitches together
st(s)	stitch(es)
St st	stockinette stitch (knit 1 row, purl 1 row; repeat)
tog	together
WS	wrong side
wyib	with yarn in back
wyif	with yarn in front
YO	yarn over needle from front to back

Bibliography

Square, Vicki. *The Knitter's Companion.* Loveland, Colo.: Interweave Press, 1996.

365 Knitting Stitches a Year: Perpetual Calendar. Woodinville, Wash.: Martingale & Company, 2002.

new and bestselling titles from

America's Best-Loved Craft & Hobby Books®

America's Best-Loved Quilt Books®

NEW RELEASES
1000 Great Quilt Blocks
Basically Brilliant Knits
Bright Quilts from Down Under
Christmas Delights
Creative Machine Stitching
Crochet for Tots
Crocheted Aran Sweaters
Cutting Corners
Everyday Embellishments
Folk Art Friends
Garden Party
Hocus Pocus!
Just Can't Cut It!
Quilter's Home: Winter, The
Sweet and Simple Baby Quilts
Time to Quilt
Today's Crochet
Traditional Quilts to Paper Piece

APPLIQUÉ
Appliquilt in the Cabin
Artful Album Quilts
Artful Appliqué
Blossoms in Winter
Color-Blend Appliqué
Sunbonnet Sue All through the Year

BABY QUILTS
Easy Paper-Pieced Baby Quilts
Even More Quilts for Baby
More Quilts for Baby
Play Quilts
Quilted Nursery, The
Quilts for Baby

HOLIDAY QUILTS & CRAFTS
Christmas Cats and Dogs
Creepy Crafty Halloween
Handcrafted Christmas, A
Make Room for Christmas Quilts
Welcome to the North Pole

HOME DECORATING
Decorated Kitchen, The
Decorated Porch, The
Dresden Fan
Gracing the Table
Make Room for Quilts
Quilts for Mantels and More
Sweet Dreams

LEARNING TO QUILT
101 Fabulous Rotary-Cut Quilts
Beyond the Blocks
Casual Quilter, The
Feathers That Fly
Joy of Quilting, The
Simple Joys of Quilting, The
Your First Quilt Book (or it should be!)

PAPER PIECING
40 Bright and Bold Paper-Pieced Blocks
50 Fabulous Paper-Pieced Stars
For the Birds
Quilter's Ark, A
Rich Traditions
Split-Diamond Dazzlers

ROTARY CUTTING
365 Quilt Blocks a Year Perpetual Calendar
Around the Block Again
Around the Block with Judy Hopkins
Fat Quarter Quilts
More Fat Quarter Quilts
Stack the Deck!
Triangle Tricks
Triangle-Free Quilts

SCRAP QUILTS
Nickel Quilts
Scrap Frenzy
Scrappy Duos
Spectacular Scraps
Strips and Strings
Successful Scrap Quilts

TOPICS IN QUILTMAKING
American Stenciled Quilts
Americana Quilts
Batik Beauties
Bed and Breakfast Quilts
Fabulous Quilts from Favorite Patterns
Frayed-Edge Fun
Patriotic Little Quilts
Reversible Quilts

CRAFTS
ABCs of Making Teddy Bears, The
Blissful Bath, The
Handcrafted Frames
Handcrafted Garden Accents
Handprint Quilts
Painted Chairs
Painted Whimsies

KNITTING & CROCHET
365 Knitting Stitches a Year Perpetual
  Calendar
Clever Knits
Crochet for Babies and Toddlers
Crocheted Sweaters
Knitted Sweaters for Every Season
Knitted Throws and More
Knitter's Book of Finishing Techniques, The
Knitter's Template, A
More Paintbox Knits
Paintbox Knits
Too Cute! Cotton Knits for Toddlers
Treasury of Rowan Knits, A
Ultimate Knitter's Guide, The

Our books are available at bookstores and your favorite craft, fabric, and yarn retailers. If you don't see the title you're looking for, visit us at **www.martingale-pub.com** or contact us at:

1-800-426-3126
International: 1-425-483-3313
Fax: 1-425-486-7596
Email: info@martingale-pub.com

For more information and a full list of our titles, visit our Web site.